EXCELLENCE

EXCELLENCE

T. H. Bell

Paula Hawkins

Henry B. Eyring

Mary Anne Q. Wood

Arthur Henry King

Irene M. Bates

Eugene England

Bruce C. Hafen

Elizabeth Haglund

Stanford Cazier

Crawford Gates

Reba L. Keele

Deseret Book Company
Salt Lake City, Utah

©1984 Deseret Book Company

All rights reserved. No part of this book may be reproduced in any form or by any means without permission in writing from the publisher, Deseret Book Company, P.O. Box 30178, Salt Lake City, Utah 84130.

Deseret Book is a registered trademark of Deseret Book Company.

First printing in paperbound edition, March 1990

Library of Congress Catalog Card Number 84-71872

ISBN 0-87579-345-2

Printed in the United States of America

10   9   8   7   6   5   4   3   2   1

CONTENTS

KEYS TO ATTAINING EXCELLENCE IN OUR LIVES

T. H. Bell

In the report of the National Commission on Excellence in Education, this prestigious body defined excellence as "performing at the outer limits of one's capacity." We should find little reason to argue with the Commission's definition. All of us should seek to reach the highest possible levels of performance limited only by ability. To do one's best is to attain fulfillment and satisfaction. To fall short of this is to squander our potential. The only way to live a rich and rewarding life is to know deep down that we have not withheld our best effort as we face the challenges and opportunities that come our way.

In my lifetime, my deepest sorrow has come to me when I have failed, knowing that I did not use the full intensity of my mind, body, and spirit to attain what I had set out to do. My greatest joy has been found in accomplishments in which I had invested my very best effort. Sometimes I have failed in spite of all the best energy and talent I could muster. In those failures, I have felt some disappointment but never the lingering remorse and self-recrimination that come from knowing I have not done my best.

To attain excellence in our lives, we must approach each task with a will to use the full limits of our talent.

We often conclude that we cannot reach high levels of accomplishment because we have not been endowed with the ability to do so. We think that we are not bright enough or that we lack the specific talent. But we seldom use our full capacities. I am reminded of a very remarkable high school girl to whom I taught chemistry.

In our small high school, the students and faculty were well acquainted. Teaching and learning were individualized and personal. This young woman came to my attention when she was in the ninth grade. We gave her several IQ tests because her achievement in school far exceeded that of many classmates who scored much higher on a highly respected intelligence test. The highest she ever scored was 97, but her achievement exceeded two very bright and talented students who had scored above 130. She was an exemplary student who utilized every opportunity and every moment of the day. Learning was not easy, especially when new and somewhat complex subject matter was being introduced, but she was very intense. She was never reluctant to ask questions nor to reveal what she did not know. She had a deep and abiding will to achieve, and exam questions missed were mastered and not missed in any subsequent test. What she lacked in brilliance she made up in effort and by steady, relentless pursuit of mastering her lessons.

This young woman graduated at the head of her class and was the valedictorian. She reached her goal to be the best because she had learned that it took her longer to learn. She knew that her steady, unrelenting effort would bring her to full mastery, if she were willing to pay the price.

I will always remember this remarkable student. She was an inspiration to the faculty and her classmates. Her example was contagious. Hers was living proof that the will to learn and the self-discipline to use time wisely and effectively will lead to success that never comes to those who, regardless of talent, hold back their best effort. A positive attitude, full commitment, and self-discipline to work hard can all compensate for endowed talent. You don't have to be bright to attain excellence. You just have to be ambitious.

Why do individuals of equal talent seem to show such vast differences in performance? What motivates some students to face adversity and failure with stubborn determination that leads to triumphant success after long periods of discouragement? What causes others to make a half-hearted attempt and then leave the challenge with an alibi? The rich inner spirit of the one who achieves seems to conquer the promptings to quit and declare the task to be impossible.

Through my many years in education, it has been my privilege to observe hundreds of students as they meet those crucial points in academic accomplishment where those with will and character meet and surmount obstacles while those prone to accept discouragement and failure use them as an excuse to gain relief from the burdens of study. Mental labor is difficult. Learning new subject matter and mastering crucial skills lead all of us to periods of self-doubt, fear of failure, and inner feelings of inadequacy. But anyone who can think can learn, if he or she will try and fail and try and fail and come back to the task again and again. What one student learns with ease, another may have to attain by paying a much steeper price in toil and effort. But those who learn with difficulty seem to appreciate their attainments—they seem to retain and utilize what was learned because it was acquired at a very dear price.

Some parents, it seems to me, have so much compassion and love for their children that they are not capable of giving them the benefit of a childhood filled with the challenges and discipline that will build strength, stubborn will, and a "can-do" attitude. To help our children attain excellence in their lives, we must discipline them and love them. We must encourage and reward them. We must forge the inner steel of a strong character by seeing that they have a healthy amount of creative tension in their lives. Too much generosity, compassion, and parental intervention and assistance will destroy the very thing most parents want for their children.

There are certain universal laws that surround all of us in our lives. If we break those laws, we must pay a price. When we meet the terms of the laws of the universe, we find the joy of accomplishment. Sometimes we deny our children character-building experiences because we love their smiles and we have understandable parental empathy for their discouragement and pain. There should be no pain for the sake of experiencing it simply in the name of character development. But there must also not be an artificial environment established by doting parents who shield their children from the normal pressures, disappointments, and defeats. If excellence in our lives means to perform at the outer limits of our ability, we must constantly test those limits for our children as well as for ourselves.

When we commit ourselves to attaining excellence in our lives, we have goals to reach, obstacles to surmount, and time-phased action steps to be executed. Living is purposeful. As our minds run over the immediate past, we feel fulfillment and satisfaction in contemplating what we have done and where we have come over the past weeks and months. Certain milestones loom up before us. We remember unexpected troubles and reversals. We recall how we adjusted our aim, revised our plan, and adopted new strategy to meet an adversarial situation.

All of this is to living what salt, pepper, and seasoning are to food. It adds flavor and interest to our days. We meet the challenges, beat down the obstacles, and stand ultimately upon a summit where we can survey our newly won terrain. This all enriches the soul. We are stronger and better and healthier in outlook, spirit, and body from the pursuit.

In our families, there must be sharing of the richness of the quest for excellence. Every member must feel the momentum of the onward march and the upward climb. This develops talent. In the process of this development, we transform ourselves to something greater, bigger, and stronger than we were. If parents fail to share this quest, they may develop themselves but deny the same to their children.

Whatever else we do with our lives, we should share our failures as well as our successes. When we fall short, there must be assessment. If this process is open to all who know us and have some stake in the positive and negative aspects of the situation, learning will lead to new aims and a renewal of resolve. Too many tend to cover up and downplay failure. We do this with our associates in our work, and we do it with members of our families. But children will learn to cope with and grow from failure if they are given a chance to see it as it is for all of us. Failures can be teaching opportunities. They can be goal-setting, purpose-revising experiences, if they are taken as they should be and if there is healthy curiosity about roots and causes.

We are all aware of the dangers of setting unrealistic, unattainable goals. We know that we can be too impatient and anxious about accomplishment. Dread of failure and shame about mistakes, neglect, and lack of preparation can lead to blame fixing, disharmony, and strife. But heroism can emerge from having failed. This is particularly true if failure is followed by careful planning, analyses of difficulties, and subsequent success. The new triumph is appreciated all the more. The lessons learned are the most precious of all. Failures can help to shape excellence in our lives, if we turn the sour taste of lemon into lemonade as we come back from defeat.

Preparation, as we all know, is a key element in success. Most failures result from lack of preparation. We are all familiar with situations where we failed to prepare and lived to regret it. Much of the misery in the world comes from poor preparation and ignorance.

Our fast-paced society seems to discourage preparation. We see advertisements and we read articles in the press and in books that emphasize the easy, effortless path to attaining what we want. We see instant success portrayed in movies and on television. There are, indeed, some shortcuts and some new approaches to old tasks that we should master, but we must beware of simplistic solutions and quick cures and remedies.

Preparation for life's challenges is a critical ingredient to attaining excellence. To live the best life and to attain the utmost from each day, month, and year of our lives, we must understand the need to prepare ourselves adequately.

It is hard to have a buoyant spirit in a tired, unhealthy, poorly conditioned body. We cannot perform at our best and to the full outer limits of our capacity unless we are physically fit, well nourished, and strong. Preparation begins with our physical bodies. Daily exercise, adequate rest, and the building of organic vigor in our bodies can make intellectual and spiritual pursuits more attainable. All of this requires intelligent understanding of ourselves and wise use of the professional services of those who help us to attain and preserve our health.

In today's world, the mind must be fully nurtured and constantly educated. It takes many years to become educated. It requires a lifetime of learning to master a profession or skill and to keep current and abreast of the emerging new knowledge and technological developments.

Youths who fail to avail themselves of our nation's many wonderful education facilities cut short their potential and forfeit their opportunity to take control of their own lives. Parents who aspire for the richest opportunities for their children must recognize that education is the golden key to the door to excellence.

The home is the first classroom, and parents are the first and most influential teachers. The best inheritance one can leave a child must include a good education.

Mastery of language and the attainment of a high level of literacy lead to disciplined thinking. We must each attain the ability to write with clarity and precision. We must learn to speak articulately through the use of a vocabulary rich enough to express our thoughts and persuade others to understand and respect us. We must be able to listen and gain the full depth of meaning from what we hear. We must read with ease, speed, and comprehension. Through reading, we add to our storehouse of personal knowledge. Our lives must be filled with rich and rewarding conversation and with reading that will uplift us and draw out the best that is within us.

To attain these ends, we must become fully educated. Everyone should have a command of the fundamentals of mathematics. This takes years of study. It requires the daily application of mathematics as we function as consumers, taxpayers, and participants in our complex economic system.

Science surrounds us in our daily living. The marvels of

nature are seen through newer and richer insight when we understand the rudiments of biology, physics, and chemistry. We are able to read and understand more about our environment, about our physical bodies, and about our health. The basic principles of science are the laws of nature, and we cannot live lives of excellence and fulfillment without a full grasp of them.

We must each be prepared to carry out the heavy responsibilities of citizenship in our society. To do this, we must understand our nation's history. We must know the story of mankind, and how our great republic emerged from the past. We must understand our government and the fundamentals of freedom under the Constitution. Our free enterprise system and how our economy works must be part of our fundamental knowledge.

We need the richness and the deep meaning of literature, art, and music in our world. We should be able to speak other languages. As our world becomes smaller, this need becomes more apparent.

From all of the above, the need for the best possible education should be obvious. All of us must dedicate ourselves to a life of learning, for we will be living in a learning society in the years to come. Through learning we learn how to learn. Through education we attain a thirst and hunger for learning. We become avid readers and constant, daily learners.

Today, educational opportunities are available to all who care enough to reach out and participate. We have the greatest system of schools and colleges in the world. Public schools are free. Private schools are a bargain for the tuition they charge. Low-cost community colleges and public and private universities are available to meet all needs and learning styles. Assistance in the form of loans, grants, and work-study opportunities is available to any adult or youth who wants to launch a new career, upgrade professional competence, master new skills, or simply acquire new knowledge of personal interest. Education in America is opportunity unlimited.

Parents should insist on the best education for their children. They must also realize that their own need for learning has not stopped. They must be living examples to their children as they bring into their homes respect for learning and honor for teachers and teaching. Children should learn early in life that excellence in education requires sacrifice and hard work, and that learning will be the key to the fulfillment and intellectual integrity they seek.

A home filled with books will not result in excellence in learning if there is no preparation and scheduled time for studying them. Strange as it may seem, many youths today are disadvantaged because of all our technological advancements. Television shows offer a thrill a minute, and radios and stereo systems add to the noisy stimulation. The microcomputer has also thrust itself into the home, as video games compete with computerized learning programs for priority time. All these marvels can be blessings turned to our advantage or they can be sources of distraction from effective learning.

Time must be scheduled for reading, quiet reflection, and conversation on what is read. Parents should read *to* their children and *with* their children. When children see their parents constantly reading, they learn the value their parents place on this activity. Despite the glamour of the electronic marvels of today, a great book in quiet contact with a curious and hungry mind is still the highest use of leisure time. Whatever other pressures there may be on our time, we must never let a significant period of time pass without reading a good book. We must be readers, and what we read should be carefully planned to help us in our quest for excellence.

Reading can be a stimulating source of conversation and intellectual growth. Issues and events in current affairs can be connected to history and great literature. What we understand, how we decide to vote, what position we take in advocacy and leadership in public affairs will all have deeper and richer meaning if we read avidly. A mind is a terrible thing to waste. We must enrich ours every day, and we must stimulate and nurture the minds of our children.

To attain excellence in our lives, we must beware of imaginings, fears, and apprehensions that rob us of perspective and drain our spiritual reservoirs. We must beware of negative brooding and projecting our minds out to anticipate all the imaginable disasters that may come down upon us.

We all need variety, perspective, change of pace, and new horizons. Without these, life can become a heavy burden, and we can find ourselves enshrouded in cynicism and sadness. We need to get out into the countryside, stop to see the sunset, listen to the sounds of nature, smell the roses, tune into one of the great symphonies of Beethoven, get ourselves off the dreadful sameness of days on end without something fresh and new and stimulating! We can learn to ski or to play tennis or golf. We can add to our interest and perspective by attending opera or ballet. All of these activities are part of drinking as deeply as possible from the cup of life. They can keep our outlook positive and our zest for living freshly renewed. Our attitudes and our emotional and mental health require activities that transcend work, home, and family responsibilities.

Only to a certain extent can we influence and extend the length of our lives. But much of what we do, how we live, and how we spend our time can influence the breadth and depth of our living. Many individuals become tired and discouraged and burn out early. They fail to practice self-renewal, as their lives settle into a deeply worn rut of humdrum routine. Those who live this way find that each day is a carbon copy of the last. Time is traded for wages. Such persons grow old, top out, and go to seed.

But the opposite can also be seen all around us. Older people who are young in spirit and outlook inspire us all by their exemplary lives and commitment to excellence. They renew themselves every day with fresh and exciting experiences. They are out on that cutting edge where creative ventures are born. They are youthful and dynamic in all that they do. Theirs are the lives of the learners, the movers, the shakers. Their activities and their creativity renew their souls, replenish their spirits, and expand their vision out to the high roads of opportunity.

Planning, goal setting, and scheduling the use of our time are essential keys to attaining excellence in our lives. We have all heard the expression: If you don't know where you are going, any road will get you there. We must be wise planners. The large goals that are of the greatest importance to us must be the objects of our planning and time-priority setting.

In today's world, others can steal our time. Our time is often occupied by the telephone, the casual caller, the unexpected visitor, and persons bent on using our time to attain their ends. We must each control our own calendars. When time is not reserved for attention to our own goals, we miss opportunities and fall short of our aspirations. Above all, we must be aware that in many ways time is our only true wealth. We need to take charge of our time if we want to be in control of our own destiny.

Many people work each day without carefully thinking through their priorities. When we study, we must ask ourselves what knowledge is of greatest worth. As we set out to do today's work, we must be satisfied that we are working at tasks that have the highest priority. If we allow others to intervene, we can find ourselves almost unwittingly working at some task that we never ever planned to occupy our time. Large goals of significance must be the mountains we climb each day. This requires disciplined thought, systematic planning, and a resolve that first things will come first every day.

To be outstandingly efficient performers who settle for nothing short of excellence, we must have dreams that turn into obsessions. We must be fanatically devoted to the accomplishment of a carefully limited number of large and meaningful goals. These goals must have been set after many months and years of reflection.

The lives of many great men and women have been dominated by obsessive devotion to accomplishment of a very few high priorities. Our goals must be bigger than ourselves. They must be lasting. They must be of such worth as to endure throughout our lifetime.

Happiness, success, and genuine excellence will crown

the efforts of dedicated, obsessively committed persons who know what they want from life. Strategy may be modified as new and more promising approaches to attaining goals emerge, but the large goals remain constant. The mountains of the mind were constructed early in life; they reflect the values and priorities that determine the main highway to be traveled all through the years of life.

We must set big goals, and cling to them when we know that they contain the enduring values and verities for us individually. Each morning we must have unfinished business that causes us to get up from our resting place with enthusiasm to further our goal-seeking journeys. That's life at its best. These are the keys to attaining excellence in our lives.

Terrel H. Bell, United States Secretary of Education in the administration of President Ronald Reagan, has been U.S. Commissioner of Education, Utah Commissioner of Higher Education, and Utah State Superintendent of Public Instruction. He received his bachelor's degree from Southern Idaho College of Education, master's degree from the University of Idaho, and Ph.D. in educational administration from the University of Utah. He was on the faculty of Utah State University and served as superintendent of two school districts in Utah. In the Church he served on the Sunday School general board and most recently as a gospel doctrine teacher. He and his wife, Betty Ruth, have four sons.

A CELEBRATION OF
AND A PLEA FOR EXCELLENCE

Senator Paula Hawkins

Excellence is a word synonymous with the gospel of Jesus Christ. As Mormons, we constantly strive to achieve the best in our pursuit. The Gentile world knows us best by our belief in work, and that is how it should be. The Mormon philosophy is one of action, of commitment and follow-through. For those who truly embrace the gospel, excellence and achievement are evident throughout their lives.

Therefore, it concerns me deeply when I encounter those who boldly question the excellence of Mormon women. Clearly no one is impugning their virtue. However, be assured that there are those who question the ability of Mormon women to make their place in today's rapidly changing world.

And, make no mistake about it, this is a double negative—one from without the Church and another from within. There are those in the world who feel Mormon women are deprived and incapable of competing in or contributing to the world. And there are those in the Church who feel that they simply are not qualified or prepared to make their way. To both groups I say nonsense! These myths need to be dispelled once and for all.

From my seat in the United States Senate I can tell you two things conclusively: there has never been a greater need for private citizen involvement in their community, and Mormon women are uniquely qualified to make a difference—and fast!

Therefore, my comments in this volume are directed to the women of the Church: a celebration of your excellence and a plea for your involvement in your world.

First, the celebration of your excellence. To give the proper perspective to this discussion, comparisons will be made with the world at large.

1. You have the serenity of knowing who you are, where you came from, why you are here, and where you are going. Precious few people in the history of this world have had this rock, this anchor in their lives. The stability you enjoy is too often minimized amid our day-to-day travail. You have a sure knowledge that you are a regal daughter of our Father in heaven. Never sell that testimony short.

2. You have embraced a religious philosophy that deals precisively with rights and wrongs. You know which decisions are proper and which are not in virtually every area of your life. There are few shades of gray in the path in which you must travel. The vast majority of people in your community do not enjoy this benefit. Most individuals are struggling daily with decisions that, to you, are literally clear as a bell. I am not saying that it's easy to live within the confines of the gospel. But this knowledge, this road map outlined by the gospel, adds clarity and resolution to your existence that most people do not enjoy.

3. Your family relationships are more stable and positive than others in your community. Statistics tell us that many of the traumas that plague society as a whole occur far less frequently in Mormon homes. Divorce, infidelity, drug abuse, runaways—while not unknown in Mormon circles, these are clearly the exception. That is not to say that everything is perfect, but it just indicates that those things which provide the very fabric of mortal existence—parents, husband, and children—are far more stable in your life.

4. You belong to one of the world's greatest training organizations. The Church of Jesus Christ of Latter-day Saints literally changes lives.

Do me a favor and take the time to respond to the following questionnaire:

	Often	Sometimes	Seldom	Never
1. Have you prepared and delivered remarks before a group of 50?	___	___	___	___
of 100?	___	___	___	___
of 200?	___	___	___	___
of more?	___	___	___	___
2. Have you served as president or an officer of an auxiliary of 50?	___	___	___	___
of 100?	___	___	___	___
of 150 or more?	___	___	___	___
3. Have you prepared an agendum for a presidency meeting?	___	___	___	___
4. Have you kept minutes and filed reports for an auxiliary?	___	___	___	___
5. Have you developed long-term goals for an auxiliary?	___	___	___	___
6. Have you achieved any of the above goals you set?	___	___	___	___
7. Have you participated in planning and coordinating meetings for multiorganizations?	___	___	___	___
8. Have you written a play or skit?	___	___	___	___
9. Have you acted in a play or skit?	___	___	___	___

	Often	Sometimes	Seldom	Never

10. Have you directed a play or skit?   — — — —

11. Have you conducted a choir?   — — — —

12. Have you sung in a choir?   — — — —

13. Have you played a solo on a musical instrument?   — — — —

14. Have you sung a solo?   — — — —

15. Have you accompanied a group on a musical instrument?   — — — —

16. Have you planned and prepared a dinner
    for 50?   — — — —
    for 100?   — — — —
    for 200 or more?   — — — —

17. Have you planned and directed a special event, such as a dance, a fair, or picnic, for a group of 50?   — — — —
    of 100?   — — — —
    of 200 or more?   — — — —

18. Have you prepared and taught an object lesson?   — — — —

19. Have you made a poster or visual aid for advertising?   — — — —

	Often	Sometimes	Seldom	Never
20. Have you planned and decorated a bulletin board?	___	___	___	___
21. Have you typed and produced a program for a meeting?	___	___	___	___
22. Have you canvassed your organization by telephone?	___	___	___	___
23. Have you mastered a skill sufficiently to teach others and then done so?	___	___	___	___

I stop here only because of space and time requirements. Obviously, this list could go on indefinitely. Please review the responses objectively. You are a multitalented and experienced individual. With a group of women like this, the world could be taken over in a day. You have had experience in vast and varied areas because of the opportunities afforded you by the Church; couple these opportunities with a little talent and the world had better look out!

The real celebration of your excellence comes when you couple the four areas discussed earlier with the zealous work so prevalent in the Mormon philosophy. When you act on your testimony, your desire to keep the commandments, your dedication to your family, and your many opportunities for service in the Church, the end product is a vital, enthusiastic, and invaluable woman, a true profile in excellence by anyone's standards.

Now for the plea (being a politician I simply can't resist this opportunity to mount my soapbox).

Sisters, export your hard-won excellence to your community. Reach out and touch your neighbors and friends. Let them see your light. Let them observe your family at work. Let them hear you speak, see you take charge of meetings, watch you organize a dinner. Let them feel your love and concern for all of God's children.

For so long, talented women like this have been almost exclusively church-centered. The result is impressive and certainly not to be maligned. But my plea is this: Stretch a little further and see what can be accomplished.

We can protect our children when they are in our homes, and we can protect them when they are at our churches, but once they are out in the community, they are on their own. And the vast majority of time in our families' day is spent away from both home and church. The community and its standards and services are becoming more and more important in the lives of Latter-day Saints, and that is as it should be.

Involvement is the only way to make sure your presence is felt. And, believe me, a very small amount of time dedicated to community service and involvement can build a lot when it is of the quality that we can give. Its benefits are myriad, including these:

First, it is good to become visible in your community. Lives centered exclusively around the Church are lives that might not be in touch with the issues that have impact on the quality of life in your community. Find out what is going on and act on that.

Second, your family will benefit dramatically from your presence in the community. Once they see your circle of friends and influence grow, they will realize that families have a vital place in the community. They will feel more welcome and accepted, and they will also feel a stronger responsibility to set the proper example at all times. I strongly feel that a family circle can never be too big.

Third, it is good for you to know just how much you have accomplished. Sometimes, judged exclusively by Mormon standards, it's not too difficult to come up short. There is always someone else who has a more detailed journal, a more complete genealogy, a neater home, better wheat bread, and a more thorough knowledge of food storage. In fact, sometimes it's easier to toss in the towel and simply give in to the pressure. However, once out in the community, you'll be surprised how very accomplished you are (please refer to the questionnaire, the answers to which we seem to take for granted). And positive reinforcement is always welcome.

Fourth, any community group or organization is going to be better for your involvement. Volunteers are at a premium. And you are reliable and well-versed in principles of stewardship. You are multitalented. And, most importantly, you have a unique vision of the world, one that truly results in a better place for us all. So inventory your personal likes and your family's needs, and choose a group to join. It may be the PTA, the symphony guild, or a local political party or group. But once your commitment is made, follow through and then monitor the results. I feel confident that you'll be pleased.

Involvement is the best and most effective way (and the easiest for those timid souls among us) to make sure our friends see what The Church of Jesus Christ of Latter-day Saints really is. Involvement is the only true way to see that myths and misinformation are dispelled once and for all. To watch our women in action is to view some of God's noblest creatures on the go. Your circle of influence will grow dramatically, and the lives you touch will be better for it.

After all, isn't this what the Savior meant when he said, "Feed my sheep"? I strongly feel that by our works he will know us. Let your excellence shine.

Paula Hawkins, a native Utahn, is United States Senator from the state of Florida. In the Senate she sits on several committees and subcommittees and chairs the Investigations and General Oversight Subcommittee under the Department of Labor and Human Resources. She sponsored and was largely responsible for passage of a bill to require the Federal Bureau of Investigation to deal with child kidnappings. A former history student at Utah State University, she has served in the Church as a stake Relief Society president. She and her husband, Gene, have three children.

EXCELLENCE IN EDUCATION

Henry B. Eyring

Letters from students come to my desk every week, testifying to the value of education. Most of those students are struggling for opportunity. They ask for help. A few ask another question: "How can I get the most from the educational opportunities I have?" They see that excellence in education will depend more on what they do than what someone else does for them. If you asked me that question, here is how I would respond.

I've learned as student and teacher to recognize three main enemies of learning. They are attitudes in the student: self-doubt, indifference, and pride. If you doubt your capacity to learn, you are right to doubt. If you don't care whether or not you learn, you won't. And if you want to learn without correction from someone else, you have chosen the harder way. But if you believe you can learn, if learning rivets your attention, and if you take counsel easily, then you can learn. And you can create for yourself excellence in education.

The best guide I know to such excellence is in a single paragraph that doesn't mention education. It was said by a prophet who lacked even the rudiments of educational opportunity, by the world's standards. And yet none of us match him in educational excellence. For you, for me, for my children, and for their children, here is the credo I would offer for education.

In the April conference of the Church in 1844, the Prophet Joseph Smith said: "It is the first principle of the Gospel to know for a certainty the Character of God, and to know that we may converse with him as one man converses with another, and that he was once a man like us; yea, that God himself, the Father of us all, dwelt on an earth, the same as Jesus Christ himself did; and I will show it from the Bible." (*Teachings of the Prophet Joseph Smith*, pages 345-46.)

That counsel, taken fully, could transform your ability to achieve educational excellence. To know God, as the Prophet advised, will produce in you attitudes that lead to educational accomplishment. Learning will come only with effort, but you will have the power to give your best effort. Others, without knowledge of God, may seem to learn well. But whatever their apparent achievements, they could have done far more. Here is why.

Of all the blocks to learning, self-doubt seems to me to be most common. As a teacher, I have learned that what first appears to be indifference is often fear of failure. Learning means trying something new. No matter how hard teachers and parents may try to give students success, to learn means trial and error. And errors can always raise the question in us: "Do I have the ability to learn this?" How might the Prophet's counsel turn those moments of failure from discouragement to a decision to try again?

I know of no better medicine for self-doubt than a testimony that you are a child of God. A child can reasonably expect to become like its father. The more you strain to understand his creations, the greater confidence you can take from being his heir. Elder Mark E. Petersen said it clearly: "Again the question comes back to what is the objective of education, and the answer must always be that education is to help us properly meet life. And what is the objective in life? . . . We are to so lay up our plans that eventually we may become like God." (Talk at Brigham Young University, February 23, 1958.)

A young man appeared in my doorway when I was the president of Ricks College. He had arrived a few days before the other students, lacking money for either a room or tuition. He stopped by to say hello and to ask if I knew how he could earn some money. He was trying college not because his family expected it of him, but because since he joined the Church his desire to learn had grown. And with it grew an understanding that he was a son of God. He found work, splitting wood. He found college work hard. He took longer to learn than others. He might reasonably have quit. But he didn't, in part because he believed Elder Petersen's instruction literally—eventually he could become like God. If he could learn any truth eventually, then one failure just told him it would take longer, not that he could not learn. That gave him patience and persistence. When he tried and couldn't understand, he tried again. In that, he was closer to genius than he would have dreamed.

Just as self-doubt is an enemy of learning, so is disinterest. Excellence in anything, but especially in learning, takes tenacity and discipline. Learning almost never yields to fits and starts of effort. It takes sustained attention. My father taught me that lesson by example and by quiet questions. A week after teaching me how to do a physics problem, he found I had forgotten the method. He was surprised and asked, "But when you walk down the street, or are in the shower, or whenever you can choose what you think about, don't you think about physics?" He urged me to choose work where my answer to that question could be "Yes." He taught me this truth: excellence in education takes absorption complete enough to shut out interruptions, diversions, and even clocks.

How can the Prophet Joseph's advice to know God help you find that power of concentration? When you know, love, and wish to emulate God, you become hungry for learning. Returned missionaries from all over the world write to me. Invariably they say, "As I served God, I came to know Him. I learned that I have covenanted to serve Him forever. And now I want to know more in preparation for my next service." They don't quote the 88th section of the Doctrine and Covenants, but they understand it:

"That you may be instructed more perfectly . . . of things both in heaven and in the earth, and under the earth; things which have been, things which are, things which must shortly come to pass; things which are at home, things which are abroad; the wars and the perplexities of the nations, and the judgments which are on the land; and a knowledge also of countries and of kingdoms— . . . that ye may be prepared in all things when I shall send you again to magnify the calling whereunto I have called you, and the mission with which I have commissioned you." (D&C 88:78-80.)

You have known students whose academic records improved sharply on their return from a mission. Part of that change is a new confidence, born of experience, that they can learn. But at least as much is a hunger to know more to serve better. I spoke at the funeral of a young man who had returned only a few years before from a foreign mission. His companions told me that on the night before he was killed, he was studying the missionary lessons in the language of the people he had taught. He could not have expected to return soon to that country, but if the gospel is taught in the spirit world in the languages of this earth, he arrived prepared. And he was prepared because his hunger to learn produced the power for sustained effort, even around a campfire on a mountainside.

If you overcome fear and indifference, you will learn. And if you learn well and compare your performance with that of others, you will likely hit against the next—and most dangerous—barrier to excellence in learning: pride. Success in learning has in it the seed of failure. But it has other seeds as well. Whether the seed of pride grows and chokes your learning will depend on how you measure your success.

We are apt to judge our success by comparison. Schools encourage that with their grading process, which is done not to educate people but to certify them. And because those who use certification want some ranking of students, your success almost surely will invite you to look down on others. That feeling of pride can close the door to learning from teachers, and even from God. Nephi taught: "O that cunning plan of the evil one! O the vainness, and the frailties, and the foolishness of men! When they are learned they think they are wise, and they hearken not unto the counsel of God, or they set it aside, supposing they know of themselves, wherefore, their wisdom is foolishness and it profiteth them not. And they shall perish." (2 Nephi 9:28.)

But the danger will be slight for you if you follow the counsel to "know for a certainty the Character of God." The source of your self-confidence in failure will also be the source of your humility in success. Your successes will be put in perspective. First, you can be sure that your efforts to approximate the truth, which is the best human learning can do, will someday be shown to be approximate. The great Sir Isaac Newton did not live to see his laws of mechanics modified by the theory of relativity, but he surely would have smiled at the arrogance of those who thought his laws so complete that man could do without God. And, second, you can be confident that a loving Father, to whom your best work is literally child's play, will be eager to help you move on to better approximations of the truth he knows perfectly.

The same scripture describes that possibility: "But to be learned is good if they hearken unto the counsels of God." (2 Nephi 9:29.) In fact, to hearken to the counsels of God is a good way to become more learned. It will take the fear out of failure, the boredom out of General Education requirements, and the risk of pride out of the honors of men.

If to know the character of God is the way to educational excellence, what should a student do about it? It will take more than academic study. You could master the multiplication facts of arithmetic and move on. But knowing God is another matter. Even those who once knew by the Holy Spirit that God lives may, after neglect, become blinded and say that there is no God. So the study you need is not primarily, or even largely, done by logical powers. And it must be continuous, so that you have recent testimony that he lives. Elder Petersen described the testimony you need:

"Every one of us must do as the Presidency of the Church does, and that is to treat God as a person and not as a concept or an idea of any kind. He is a *person*, and we need to deal with Him that way. We must realize that He has feelings, and we can offend Him or we can please Him, depending on our attitude." (Address at Brigham Young University, September 1, 1983.)

You can know God best as a person by communicating with him and serving him. That cannot be done primarily in a classroom, nor is it easily assigned by a teacher. You will need to pray, to fast, and to ponder the scriptures. The effort and its results are described in this instruction:

"Humble yourselves before the Lord, and call on his holy name, and watch and pray continually, that ye may not be tempted above that which ye can bear, and thus be led by the Holy Spirit, becoming humble, meek, submissive, patient, full of love and all long-suffering; having faith on the Lord; having a hope that ye shall receive eternal life; having the love of God always in your hearts, that ye may be lifted up at the last day and enter into his rest." (Alma 13:28-29.)

The first responsibility must be yours, not a teacher's. And yet two things can happen to you from attending a class regularly that you aren't likely to find alone. First, you can gain confidence from the expressed testimonies of your teacher and classmates. Coming to know God has moments of discouragement, like any learning. A teacher or a fellow student who bears testimony that prayers are answered, for example, can help you keep trying, when the heavens may seem closed to you. Second, your desire to contribute to a regular and frequent class discussion can spur the scripture study without which you cannot stay close to God.

If you make knowing God and serving him the center of your education, you will gain the attitudes necessary to learn as well as you can. And that is excellence. It will not end all failure, but it will reduce the fear and self-doubt that failure can produce. It will not make every lecture interesting, but it will help you find ideas and feelings in them that matter enough to engage your full attention. And it will not blind you to comparisons with others, but comparison with the majesty of God will take care of pride. As you come to know God better, you will appreciate more the teachers who nurture your testimony of God and his prophets, not only as a part of your education but as the heart of it.

Henry B. Eyring was born and reared in New Jersey, where his father, Henry Eyring, was a professor of chemistry at Princeton University. After receiving degrees from the University of Utah and Harvard University, he was a professor at the Graduate School of Business at Stanford University. He subsequently became president of Ricks College and then Deputy Commissioner of Education for the Church. He is presently Commissioner of the Church Educational System. Dr. Eyring has been a bishop and member of the Sunday School general board. He is married to the former Kathleen Johnson, and they are parents of four sons and two daughters.

THE MORE EXCELLENT WAY

Mary Anne Q. Wood

On a cold December day in 1847, a baby girl named Mahala Elmer was born in Boxford, Suffolk, England. Her father, a maker of fine shoes, maintained his family in comfortable circumstances. Six years later, however, he died, leaving the mother and five small children. The mother, deserted by her family and friends because she had joined The Church of Jesus Christ of Latter-day Saints and unable to continue her husband's trade, was forced to separate the family. At the tender age of eight, Mahala was apprenticed to a tailoress.

The tailoress provided Mahala with food and shelter and gave her instruction in the trade, but she was not kind to her and compelled her to work very hard. Mahala never again lived in her mother's home except for one all too brief three-week period when she had the measles and her employer sent her home to the care of her mother.

For Mahala, the only bright spot in the tailoress's household was a sympathetic grandmother. When Mahala was sixteen years old, this grandmother helped her to run away, but she was forced to return when she found she could not secure other employment without her service papers. Finally the grandmother convinced the tailoress to give Mahala her papers, and she left to find employment in household service. In one home she was taught to read the Bible, and on another occasion the Mormon elders helped her learn to write. These were her only opportunities for formal education.

From her meager wages, Mahala saved enough money to permit her family to emigrate to Zion in 1870. Shortly after her arrival, she became the fourth wife of Thomas Jenkins, the bishop of the Fourth Ward of Salt Lake City, and embarked on a life of service to home and community. She was secretary and treasurer of the Relief Society, a Relief Society teacher, president of the Primary, a Sunday School teacher, and, for many years, a counselor to the president of the Relief Society. Her special task was to prepare those who had died for burial, a task she performed at all hours of the day and night and under many trying circumstances. On one occasion, she went into the home of a non-Mormon family where a child had died of a contagious disease. Others refused to go and tend to the dead, but Mahala went and prepared the child for burial. When she returned home, she had her children throw her clothes outdoors to her, and she washed and changed in the coal shed so that she would not expose her children to the dreaded illness.

Because Mahala had only limited opportunities for education herself, she was anxious that her children have the opportunities that she had been denied. Through her sacrifice and insistence, her children received educations beyond those that were the common privilege in her day. When the children were raised, Mahala turned her talents to assisting with the rearing of her grandchildren. Her relations with these grandchildren were touching and beautiful. She never kept anything for herself but gave everything away.

On her death, one of her sons-in-law, Carlos Badger, paid her the following tribute:

In all the relations of life, she expressed her personality, to use the terms of modern psychology, through service to others. She had no self-centered aspirations. As long as she could be occupied from early until late in doing things for others, she was happy. To use her strength in practical routine of duties was her only ambition. Denied intellectual interests, in the narrow sense of the words, she occupied her time in service for others and in self-sacrifice. The idea of duty, which seems almost repugnant to some who regard themselves as moderns, was to her a joy and a delight. Her whole life cries shame upon the selfish, shallow ideas of those who waste their time in petty personal desires, consulting their own circumstances, their own likes and dislikes, their own comfort. She was strong, but not for selfish interests; insistent, but not upon whims and mere fancies; tireless, but for the good of others. Life lost its zest and flair only when she could not bear heavy burdens for others around her. . . . Her life from its humble beginning, with what we might regard as limited opportunities, is a solemn warning to those who knew her that opportunity is more than house and lands, worldly place and position, college degrees and titles.

Mahala Elmer Jenkins was my great-grandmother. Ever since I read her story some years ago, I have regarded her life as the essence of excellence, because she learned to work hard, she set high standards for herself, and she lived so that her life enriched all who came in contact with her. Although her life was devoid of the kind of opportunities for education, wealth, and position that many today would regard as essential, Mahala Jenkins found the excellent way. Many lessons about excellence can be learned from the life of this small and obscure pioneer woman.

Excellence in life does not demand exceptional opportunities; instead, even limited opportunities must be treated exceptionally. Too often we confuse excellence with prominence, forgetting that the most excellent life of all, the life of the Savior, was spent as a carpenter and preacher without worldly possessions or position. Most examples of excellence never appear in history books or in the newspapers nor are they discussed on the television or the radio. The conscientious parent, the careful professional, the skilled tradesman may never achieve recognition outside their immediate circle, but their standards of excellence enrich all who come in contact with them.

Excellence for most people does not mean doing great and heroic deeds. Rather, it means doing little, routine, and mundane things well. In this regard, life is like the Bayeux Tapestry, one of the largest and most aesthetically pleasing pieces of narrative art in the world, which tells the story of William the Conqueror. The tapestry is 20 inches wide and

231 feet long and is divided into 79 panels, each telling a different story. The tapestry is made from eight shades of woolen yarn embroidered on linen cloth. Millions of simple routine stitches were carefully placed in the cloth to make this masterpiece, just as millions of routine acts can make an excellent life.

Perhaps one author summed up excellence best when he said, "Whate'er thou art, act well thy part." But this is easier said than done. It is one thing to give all our effort to a starring role, and quite another to give our all to a bit part or a job behind the scenes.

Mahala Jenkins's visiting teaching is one example of her excellent life. One of her granddaughters has reported that Mahala was a faithful visiting teacher most of her adult life. The grandchildren remember her visiting every home on the block, bustling back and forth between her neighbors' houses and her home to deliver soup or bread or other items required to meet the needs of those whom she visited.

To some, making the effort to be an excellent home teacher or visiting teacher may not seem as important as making the effort to be an excellent bishop or Relief Society president. But the irony is that we will be judged here and hereafter on our excellence in small as well as great opportunities. The commendation of the Lord to the faithful servant in the parable of the talents is very apt: "Well done, thou good and faithful servant: thou hast been faithful over a few things, I will make thee ruler over many things." (Matthew 25:21.) Moreover, our capacity to take advantage of large opportunities may well be dictated by our excellence in small ones. Doctrine and Covenants 64:33 reads: "Wherefore, be not weary in well-doing, for ye are laying the foundation of a great work. And out of small things proceedeth that which is great." In other words, excellence can become a habit.

Developing the habit of excellence takes consistent effort. Many individuals can marshal their resources for an initial effort in the direction of excellence, but it is far more difficult to strive consistently for excellence.

Recently, I read the following in an advertisement for

the McDonald's Corporation. It was entitled "Press On." "Nothing in the world can take the place of persistence. Talent will not; nothing is more common than unsuccessful men with talent. Genius will not; unrewarded genius is almost a proverb. Education alone will not; the world is full of educated derelicts. Persistence and determination alone are omnipotent." Despite the importance of persistence and determination, such qualities are rare.

Every year I watch with some interest as a group of students enters the law school where I teach. Most of them begin with enthusiasm, working hard to be prepared for class, striving to do well. Then some start compromising on their daily preparation. After the first set of exams, others become discouraged and blame the system for their failure to do as well as they had hoped. Many quit preparing consistently and start using commercially prepared briefs and outlines instead of reading cases and briefing them themselves. They settle into a routine designed to "get them through" the next three years until they can graduate.

Fortunately, there are other students who continue to seek excellence. Some of them receive good grades, which adds to their motivation for continued effort. But the students whom I admire most are the ones who seek excellence through consistent daily preparation even though they do not immediately achieve the recognition for their efforts that they no doubt would desire.

I remember a very fine young man in one of the first classes I taught. He was always well-prepared, and his excellent comments and questions in class contributed to the classroom experience of every student. His first semester grades were a disappointment, and I am sure he was unhappy when he did not complete the first year of law school in the top ten percent and make the law review. But he came back the next year with the same high standards of preparation. Eventually his grades improved, and by the end of his three years he graduated in the top ten percent and found a job with a very fine law firm. I would never hesitate to recommend to anyone that they take their legal problems to such a person, because I know he had developed the habit of excellence and would persevere no matter what difficulties were encountered.

Excellence requires more than persistence; it also requires vision. As we strive for eternal life, it is important that each one of us keep our eye trained on the objective: to live a Christ-like life. To the extent that we strive to know and to emulate the Savior, we will have a vision constantly before us of the objective. This is true as we strive to achieve excellence in any endeavor. Recently I read an article about champion ice skaters who prepare for competition by spending time every day visualizing themselves performing their skating routines flawlessly. This type of mental preparation helps them excel when they are performing on the ice. If we can visualize an excellent performance, we are more likely to give an excellence performance.

Not long ago I had a conversation with the great Western artist, Ed Fraughton, whose work appears in galleries throughout the United States and who was at the time working on a seventeen-foot-high statue of a rider on a bucking horse, which is to be displayed in the state capitol of Wyoming. In the room he had a small model of the statue he was carving. He said that the first time he won a commission to do a life-sized sculpture, he worked it up in a very small model, and someone asked him how he was going to construct the full-sized statue. He replied, "I am going to make it just like this, only twelve times bigger." At the time, he reports, he did not have any idea how he was going to accomplish that task. Mr. Fraughton could visualize his small model twelve times larger, though, and this vision helped him achieve his goal.

Like Ed Fraughton's clay model, we can seek out models of excellence to broaden our vision. Before I entered law school, I read the biographies of several great American lawyers. I remember particularly the story of John Adams's courageous defense of the British soldiers accused in the Boston Massacre. Such stories helped me to visualize what it means to be an excellent lawyer.

Having a vision of excellence does not necessarily mean that we can only be satisfied with perfection. Excellence is not perfection. And while perfection may be a worthy long-term objective, the desire for perfection in the short term can be paralyzing. The search for excellence demands the ability to know how and where to compromise and accept some performances that are less than perfect. In 1961 General George B. McClellan was named Commander of the Army of the Potomac by President Lincoln. At the time of his appointment he wrote his wife, "The people call upon me to save the country. I must save it." During the early months of his command, McClellan was a hero and was called the "Young Napoleon." He trained, drilled, and marched his troops, but he never engaged them in combat. Despite Lincoln's urging, McClellan refused to attack the Confederate forces. He always needed more men and more training. Finally he was relieved of his command and others were called upon to save the union. McClellan's desire for a perfect army prevented the army from doing its job.

In the search for excellence, not only must we be satisfied sometimes with less than perfection; we must also be able to look forward rather than backward. Many people let the disappointments and mistakes of the past keep them from achieving excellence in the present. The newspapers are full of stories of failed lives that are explained in part by abuse, bad habits, and disappointed expectations. Benedict Arnold betrayed his country in part because he was frustrated by slow promotions. Thomas B. Marsh left the Church because he could not get over a neighborhood quarrel. Richard Nixon lost the U.S. presidency because he could not say, "I am sorry." However, the principle of repentance teaches us that we need not be limited in the future by our failure to achieve excellence in the past. Mahala Jenkins was a person who learned to overcome her past. She suffered the kind of neglect as a child that often stifles the spirit. However, her spirit soared and she maintained a vision of excellence rather than a memory of a flawed past.

Our vision is clearest when our desire for excellence is motivated by unselfish interests. No doubt it is possible to do things very well while operating with very selfish motives. But true excellence is not achieved unless our efforts are motivated by love and concern for others as well as ourselves. Satchel Paige, the great black American baseball pitcher, is quoted as saying, "Never forget that there is always something greater than you are."

This principle is illustrated in the life of George Washington. He was a successful general and leader because he was able to put the interests of others and the cause of liberty above his own interests. Early in the war Washington was given a letter that General Lee, his senior division commander, had sent to Washington's adjutant general. Assuming the letter was official business, Washington opened the letter in the absence of his adjutant general. The letter, however, was a personal letter highly critical of General Washington, which made plain that the two individuals had corresponded previously along a similar vein. A lesser man might have reacted from anger and lost the services of both the offending parties. General Washington, though, knowing that the cause of liberty needed the skills of these knowledgeable though personally disloyal officers, sat down and wrote a letter to his adjutant general explaining how the letter had come into his hands. Nothing more was said about the matter. The cause was greater than his own feelings. On another occasion, Congress passed laws giving Washington increased authority. A lesser man might have used his increased authority to further his own ambitions, but Washington was concerned about the greater good. He stated, "Instead of thinking myself freed from all civil obligation by this mark of confidence, I shall constantly bear in mind that as the sword was the last resort for the preservation of our liberties, so it ought to be the first to be laid aside when those liberties are firmly established."

Washington was motivated by a cause and an interest in others greater than himself. When purely selfish interests motivate our actions, our vision is too limited to achieve true excellence. Concern for others expands our vision so that excellence is in fact possible.

George Washington has been an example of excellence

for generations. As the dominant player in one of the most significant events in world history, he is a hero on the grand scale. Today there are other individuals living excellent lives who may have a similar influence on future generations. Most people who achieve excellence, however, will be like Mahala Jenkins. Doing their best, working with high standards and limited opportunities, they will bless and enrich the lives of their families, neighbors, and associates. All of us are capable of achieving excellence on this scale, and that is all that really matters. Plutarch said, "Real excellence . . . is most recognized when most openly looked into; and in really good men, nothing which meets the eyes of external observers so truly deserves their admiration, as their daily common life does that of their nearer friends."

Mary Anne Q. Wood is a professor in the J. Reuben Clark Law School at Brigham Young University. She received a bachelor of arts in English from BYU and graduate degrees in law from the University of Utah and the National Law Center at George Washington University. In 1981-82 she was a White House Fellow under U.S. Secretary of Defense Casper Weinberger. She has served on the Utah County Merit Council, Governor's Commission on the Agenda for the Eighties, and Defense Advisory Committee on Women in the Military. Dr. Wood served a mission to the Central States and has taught in auxiliaries of the Church. She and her husband, Stephen G. Wood, have five children.

THE PURSUIT OF EXCELLENCE

Arthur Henry King

"For wisdom is a defence, and money is a defence: but the excellency of knowledge is, that wisdom giveth life to them that have it." (Ecclesiastes 7:12.) "I am come that they might have life, and that they might have it more abundantly." (John 10:10.)

It looks as if the expression "pursuit of excellence" is modeled on that most famous of phrases from that famous document "the pursuit of happiness." But is happiness something that can be pursued, or is it not rather something that happens to one? Can we pursue education in order to get education, or do we not rather do certain things that are traditionally known to produce educated men and women and hope that as a result of doing those things we may prove to be educated? Such things include training in manners, speaking, reading, writing, a foreign language, athletics, and so on.

We might ask ourselves whether indeed one can pursue anything directly except righteousness. If we were to pursue anything but righteousness, would not that pursuit get in the way of the pursuit of righteousness? Is it not task enough in life to seek to do the right thing every moment? Is this not what the gospel means when it says, "But seek ye first the kingdom of God, and his righteousness; and all these things shall be added unto you" (Matthew 6:33)?

Having cleared our minds a little about the word *pursuit* and its association with such things as hunting and gain, it is appropriate to turn to the word *excellence* and consider its re-

35

lation to competition. We are most familiar with the idea of competition in economic and athletic fields. Historically, competition in all forms of sport was originally a form of training for war. We look in vain in the scriptures for any account of "games" as we find it in the Greek and Roman tradition. From that tradition of games in Greece and Rome and from a parallel tradition in northern Europe sprang the habit of chivalric tournaments in the Middle Ages (and their relevance to war is clear). Football would appear to have begun as a competition to get hold of the head of the sacrificed animal. No doubt competition in its most extreme form in our ordinary life comes about in the playing of games and in the watching of them, in which the lowest of human urges as well as higher ones may be present. Not infrequently, the end of the most famous football match in Britain is followed by fights in which one or more people may be killed. One can sometimes hear profanity from Mormon fathers watching a basketball tournament when such fathers never in their lives otherwise utter a bad word. The practice of fouls is built into the game, and rules are made for them. Can it be regarded as the Christian thing to do to "foul" deliberately? I note with apprehension that the words *aggression* or *aggressive* can be used in the United States as terms of praise—for example, in salesmanship. Much has been said about the development of the spirit of sportsmanship, but it would be perhaps nearer the truth to say that the tradition of the playing of games throughout history has been accompanied by strong manifestations of aggressiveness, and we see in this the link with the use of games as a preparation for war.

But is not the spirit of aggressiveness rather than the spirit of sportsmanship very much to the fore also in intellectual games, such as chess? Is not the confrontation of a western chess expert with a Soviet Union player accompanied by an acute sense of feeling akin to war? I myself was a keen chess player as an adolescent and young man, and I know that sense of urgency and tension that grows as the game becomes more complex and the desire to win more strong. I also know perfectly well that unless I had the desire to win, it was less likely that I would do well. But may we not say that as intellectual an exercise as chess is, it is at its best not when we are playing a game in competition against someone else, but when we are studying a chess problem (perhaps two or three of us together) as a means of trying to solve it? Is it not here that we come down to the point at which we can separate the idea of competition from the idea of excellence?

We have now entered a field of inquiry in which we can link up the playing of intellectual games with the pursuit of research and the pursuit of the arts. In this field, competition is at its most Christian when it is a competition of oneself against oneself, the measuring of oneself against oneself, the effort to do better than one has done before. In the image of the artist dealing with his material, we have another good image of competition: not competition against our fellowmen, but collaboration with our fellowman in order to get something done. The artist may be isolated in his pursuit of excellence, although, of course, artists are in the habit of discussing among themselves and have an intense interest in one another's work—that was why Paris was such a valuable center for art in the late nineteenth and early twentieth centuries. But at the same time we need to bear in mind such efforts as those to reach the Arctic or Antarctic poles, or to climb Everest, or any other effort that involves the combination of intellect, planning, will, and love of one's fellowman. All such elements come into play when men or women combine as a team to get something of excellence done.

The artist struggles with his material whether it be stone or paint or the pencil; the architect struggles (and this may be a greater struggle) with the combination of beauty and the site that has been chosen and the use that is to be made of the building. The musician struggles with the quality of the instruments he is considering and the ability of men to play them and to play what he writes. The poet, above all, has to struggle with words, perhaps the most difficult medium of all, because words issue from the human mind itself and therefore move about and change in a way that stone and paint do not.

Paul, in his image of running a race, is not thinking of a man beating his fellowman, but of a man running the race to achieve righteousness in his life, in his conduct, in his worship.

Perhaps, then, we could sum up the phrase "the pursuit of excellence" as the pursuit of an always higher stage of achievement, not against our fellowmen but *with* our fellowmen and *for* our fellowmen; that is to say, eternal progression is ultimately an eternal progression in love from which issues the production of that which is good, that which is true, that which is beautiful, and the love of those things, and above all, of the Lord, who gives us the power under his wing to produce these things.

How, then, may we approach excellence? From our discussion above, excellence is not to be pursued in itself, but is to be pursued in conduct and in the details of conduct, in art and in the details of art, in all skills and in the details of those skills. May I give some examples of steps to excellence that are of importance in the Church.

First of all, in an approach to excellence in anything, we have to consider what has been done before us so that we may see and hear and read and know. Perhaps the most important step toward excellence is to know the scriptures well. That is something that can be begun early under the guidance of parents, who have to take the initiative. A family that reads the scriptures together regularly from the time the oldest child is still an infant in arms will be helping the children as they grow to learn the language of the scriptures at the same time as they learn their own language—to learn the language of the scriptures as a part of their own language. I'm not speaking here in the abstract; I'm speaking of what I myself have known as a child in growing up, because my father read us the scriptures every day and I became familiar with the language of the scriptures as part of my ordinary language. I will not say that I understood it immediately, but that I absorbed it and gradually came to understand it in the way that I came to understand other parts of my own language. The language of the King James Version can be built into the life of the child if it is part of his daily existence. As he hears the scriptures in the loved voices of his father and mother, he comes through that love to understand the scriptures and appreciate them in the best way. I remember still the voice of my father as he read to me the story of the calling of Samuel (a story that may appeal to a very young child, although he may not yet fully understand any more than Samuel did what it was all about).

Excellence in the sense of excelling oneself year after year in one's understanding of the scriptures is surely an excellence that has to be pursued by every member of the Church.

Another important step toward achieving excellence that today is more or less ignored in education, and yet that needs to be inculcated into the child by collaboration between the parents and the school, is to get the child used to doing routine hard work as a preparation for being able to enjoy something. It takes routine hard work for a child to learn manual skills as well as intellectual skills, and he needs to learn both. He needs to learn manual skills so that his hand and body may be trained, and through that training, further to develop and train his brain, for the channel is not simply from the brain to the hand but also from the hand to the brain. And we need to maintain the balance between mechanical and craft skills. A child who has learned to carve wood has done something more subtle than a boy who has learned to make elementary repairs on his father's car. By all means let both boy and girl learn how to repair the machines that are used about the home, but remember that the creation of things in a medium is more important than the power to repair machines. Children need to learn that a great deal of hard work lies behind the ability to enjoy doing things of importance.

In the American culture, the boy usually wants to learn how to put the ball into the basket—and his surrounding society and above all his father approve of that effort. But suppose that parents approved of other skills too, like that of learning a foreign language or of learning a musical instrument; then that child would have a fuller and richer development. Excellence in learning a foreign language is achieved by concentrating on difficult things, and with an intelligent child, that means concentrating on the difficult things first. Professor J. R. Firth used to say to me that if you are prepared to tackle the verb system of a language first (and that is usually the most difficult part), you can get ahead with that language far more quickly. Everybody knows the kind of intensive training and intensive routine work required in acquiring the power to dance or the power to play a musical instrument or the power to wield a brush or a pencil.

For the child to be prepared to learn the value of routine hard work, of "grind," he must develop an enthusiasm for something (and remember that that word itself means originally a state of being seized by God). When my stepchild came to live with us at the age of eleven, there was a problem for some months of what she could be enthusiastic about in her change of life. We found the solution: she learned to ride well and developed courage about tackling that problem on a full-size horse. When in my widowerhood I lived in my sister's family, one of my comforts when I was not at the office was to listen to my nephew at the piano. He would play a passage, record it, listen, play and record it again, listen again, and perhaps spend a whole morning working on just one passage. That required great enthusiasm in order to be able to excel. But once he had treated key passages or perhaps even the whole texture of a work in that way (it might, for example, be a piano concerto), then when he came to play that piece in public he was ready to do one of a number of different things. Where there is enthusiasm (and that is just another name for passionate love of a subject), the effort can be untiring and the end a complete spontaneity that comes only from the most complete practice. It is the ability to do anything at the moment offered. That moment may be on the concert platform or it may be a moment presented to the teacher in his class. The patience to achieve is part of the passion to achieve.

I heard Arthur Rubinstein play at the very end of his long life Schumann's *Scenes from Childhood*. In the bad sense, old age may return to childhood in imbecility. But in the good sense, old age may turn to childhood in the ultimate simplicity that comes from a hard struggle throughout a whole lifetime. Here was Rubinstein playing his life's experience into not the meretriciousness of Liszt, but the simplicity of Schumann. The ultimate excellence, which comes from all that hard work and all that hard experience, is the ultimate simplicity. The excellence of the gospel is a model for all excellence. The gospel represents that ultimate simplicity which some people may have by gift and some children bring into the world and keep. But most of us have to work hard to get back to it.

The excellence of which I speak can be most readily understood by most of us in words, in what has traditionally been called the *sermo humilis,* the plain style, the simple style, the style in which Augustine thought the scriptures should be written and taught. We find it in the greatest of nonscriptural writers in Act 4, scene 7, of *King Lear* in Cordelia's simple replies to her father's anxiety:

> Do not laugh at me;
> For, as I am a man, I think this lady
> To be my child Cordelia.
> *Cordelia.* And so I am, I am.
> *Lear.* Be your tears wet? yes, faith. I pray, weep not:
> If you have poison for me, I will drink it.
> I know you do not love me; for your sisters
> Have, as I do remember, done me wrong:
> You have some cause, they have not.
> *Cordelia.* No cause, no cause.

Let us think also of St. John, chapter 14. I would hope to be able on my deathbed to hear his words or repeat them to myself. This is the more excellent way of which Paul speaks.

The more excellent way is not the way of competition for gain or competition in skill, whether of mind or body. There is another sense of competition, which is that of seeking together. Eternal progression is not that of an isolated individual; it is that of working together in love with our fellowmen.

Harry Abrahams worked out how to win the race; Eric Liddell ran for love and to the glory of God. Abrahams lived to ripe years and had much influence in the athletic world; Liddell became a missionary in China and was martyred in early middle age. Which was the more excellent way?

Arthur Henry King is professor of English (emeritus) at Brigham Young University. Before joining the BYU faculty in 1971, he was associated with the British Council for Cultural and Educational Relations Overseas. Among his assignments with that organization were assistant director general, controller of education, and representative to Pakistan, Sweden, Belgium, and Iran. He also taught at Lund and Stockholm universities in Sweden. In the Church Dr. King has served as counselor in a branch presidency in England, high councilor, and gospel doctrine teacher. He has written and published extensively on sixteenth and seventeenth century English literature and English as a foreign or second language.

MY DANCE WITH EXCELLENCE

Irene M. Bates

The love of my young life was dancing. When I was about five years old, alone in the house except for my mother, I would fling off my clothes and dance my heart out. So Mother sent me to ballet school. The training at first tended to curb the spontaneity, and it was quite some time before I began to realize that the discipline could give me a more refined medium of expression. By the time I was nine or ten years old, dancing had become my whole life. I was a shy little girl, and, perhaps because dancing liberated something in me, I became a good dancer, pouring heart and soul into whatever was required of me. But my ballet class met on Saturday mornings. When I started work at age fourteen as a shorthand-typist, all that came to an end. I didn't know that my taste of self-expression awoke a need that never died. It simply slept for twenty years.

In 1955 when Bill and I first met the missionaries, we had been happily married fourteen years and had four lively children. My whole world was my family. I saw myself solely in terms of my roles as wife and mother, measuring myself only by the quality and quantity of service I could supply in responding to the needs of loved ones. And I was happy. Any personal longings were barely conscious, but they had something to do with a need to express myself, to discover what was there inside. (If it did touch my consciousness, it came in an image of dance.) When Bill and I joined the Church, that small slumbering hunger awakened. It has continued through our years in the Church. I can explain it only by relating some of my experiences since that time and in so doing perhaps reveal the evolution of my thinking about the idea of excellence.

After investigating the gospel for nine months, my husband and I were baptized. The most important part of our conversion was our recognition of the magnitude and intelligence of God's love and that of his Son, Jesus Christ. I remember trying to describe my feelings in the light of that revelation. I wrote it all down and gave it to one of the missionaries who had first talked with us. He was a sensitive young man who did not laugh at the idea of a thirty-four-year-old mother of four longing to dance on a green hill with the wind in her hair. Instead, he understood and was touched by the obvious deep yearning within me for some kind of spiritual expression.

Going to church after that was like going to ballet school in a way. The discipline of capturing that liberated spirit and channeling it, using it constructively, was difficult at first. Giving a talk only made me aware of the clumsy, heavy-handedness of words, and my first attempt ended in my lamely giving up. As an MIA teacher I groped for further discovery and for ways of expressing what I felt, seeking to help those young girls do the same. Not all of the programs and manuals reached us in the mission field. Some that did seemed too strange to take seriously. The Spirit was the important thing, and there were many awkward, if moving, attempts to communicate on that level. But progress came incidentally, and slowly I began to see purpose in the framework of the institution as we struggled with each new challenge, digging yet deeper for our honest responses. And there in the realm of ideas and spiritual values I began on the long and often difficult journey of discovering who I was, what I valued, and what I stood for. In the process I was finding ways too, however inadequate, of expressing those essential truths that were beginning to unfold for me.

This kind of experience was mirrored in many of the converts I knew. I saw people bloom, trying to answer to the love of God within them. There were people like Eileen

Weightman, who told me when she joined the Church that her only talent was with a scrubbing brush. She became not only a much-loved ward MIA president but later an enthusiastic, dedicated, and accomplished stake leader. There was Maureen Hoyle, a former mill-girl. She became a stake Relief Society president whose spiritual sensitivity combined with a love of the scriptures in an intelligent compassion. Then there was Doris Webb. Doris, who was in her middle years, had been a member of the Church for some time without ever having had the courage to accept an assignment. She was my visiting teaching companion, and I grew to admire her honest thinking and to enjoy her sense of humor. She loved poetry, loved words, and had so much of their beauty on the tip of her tongue that I lamented her inability to share it. When I became ward Relief Society president, I begged her to accept the calling of visiting teaching message leader. I reminded her of the enrichment her ready access to poetry could bring, and she finally consented. I will never forget seeing her teach that first time. In the beginning she was nervous, but slowly her grace and dignity and confidence emerged, freed by her love and enthusiasm for the subject.

Each of these women achieved excellence. But they accomplished it by expressing themselves and their love, more than by seeking excellence. If, in fact, excellence had been their prescribed goal, they may well have given up, thinking it beyond them. Most of my experience in the Church at that time demonstrated excellence to be a by-product rather than a sought-after end.

When we immigrated to Utah in 1967, I missed seeing this kind of transformation. I missed, too, the vitality of the mission setting where so much activity was inner-directed. Church experience in Salt Lake City was both less challenging and more challenging. Few people appeared to be searching for answers, and I still had plenty of questions aching to be asked. To ask them in such a setting suggested an attack on the faith. After a few months I was depressed, feeling guilty and ungrateful for having such feelings. It was not that there was not enough to occupy my time; even with our family grown to near-independence, there was always something to do, but busyness could not conceal a growing sense of mental and spiritual sterility. I was building up a store of book knowledge but had nowhere to go with it, no chance to test it. I felt myself becoming a Dead Sea. My stint as a Pink Lady failed to convince me I was offering any needed service, except in the case of an elderly man whom I continued to visit when he was transferred to the county hospital (no Pink Ladies graced those halls, where they were so sorely needed). But the old longings to discover my own truths, which the Church had reawakened, seemed all the more painful in my isolated capsules of home and car.

Then my daughter, Lynda, gave me a wonderful gift. Sensing my hungry unhappiness, she enrolled me in the undergraduate program at the University of Utah and then shamed, bullied, and loved me past the terror of that first day on campus. Not only was I in a new land, I had never even attended high school; and the generation gap was huge. Within hours, though, I could feel the stirrings of something coming to life again. It was a totally invigorating experience, and those generous young people made me feel completely at home. When we moved to California a year later, I attended Santa Monica College for two semesters, then went on to UCLA as a sociology major.

During my years in college the occasional "excellent" on my papers represented dabs of icing on an already rich and satisfying cake. My treasure hunts in the libraries, the thrilling discoveries that buried old preconceptions, the challenges and inner confrontations, the entrée to the brilliant minds of scholars formerly just names to me—all these were enjoyable parts of a discipline that honed my thinking. I was fortunate in being able to attend college in my fifties because, unlike the majority of students I encountered, little was at stake for me. My future was not tied up in grades, so I was able to enjoy every minute of the experience for its own sake. It was not necessary for me to juggle classes, a part-time job, and children, as many of my classmates did. Bill's delight equaled my own. I found myself walking on campus with winged feet, my spirit dancing with the sheer exhilaration and sense of freedom that each day brought. The pain that accompanied such growth was a price I was willing to pay. Fine teachers encouraged the discovery of some of the most significant revelations of my intellectual life, experiences that are central to my personal definition of excellence. Let me share two.

The first came from David Shibley of Santa Monica College. In an American history class already fully weighted with reading and other assignments, he challenged the students to undertake one more. He asked us to evaluate a politician by reading many contradictory analyses (the reading list was two pages long). Furthermore, the sizeable paper would not add to our grade if we did a good job, and might even lower it. He wanted us to do this exercise purely for the experience and for our "pleasure." The young people in the class, already anxious about grades, did not accept the invitation. I was the only one able to afford the challenge, and I was tempted largely because Franklin D. Roosevelt was the figure in question.

After several weeks of reading on top of a full load of other courses, I discovered that I was obsessed. I could think of nothing else. When the final two weeks of the semester arrived, I went to Mr. Shibley's office and confessed that I could not set aside my own bias in favor of FDR—a hero of my World War II experience in England. I found myself constantly defending him. After listening to my apologies, Mr. Shibley smiled broadly, sat back in his chair, and told me this was the whole purpose of the project. As writers he wanted us to be aware of the difficulty of dealing with our own biases or values, and as readers he wanted us to know they exist in others. Because of this exercise he felt we might be more understanding of writers' problems, but also a little more critical of what we read. By forcing me to confront the elusiveness of truth in history, Mr. Shibley had made the responsibility mine—to search and to evaluate. Even excellence, a by-product of that process, would be personal, dependent upon an internal recognition of truth that must validate whatever evidence was presented.

I will always be grateful to Mr. Shibley for giving me the opportunity of learning that lesson firsthand. Yet even so valuable a lesson has its limitations. In a seminar in sociological theory at UCLA, along with other requirements, we were asked to address various long-standing debates. Mine was an argument arising from an essay by Max Weber, "The Meaning of Ethical Neutrality in Sociology and Economics." Several eminent sociologists over the years had taken Weber to task for urging value-free sociology, which, his critics maintained, was at worst impossible and at best undesirable. I heartily agreed with Weber's critics. Objectivity *was* impossible in the social sciences. Along with the other students in the seminar, I was required to produce a twenty- to thirty-page paper analyzing the various positions in the debate, then an appendix containing my personal judgment based upon the readings, using reasoning and personal experience, if possible, to substantiate my conclusions.

On the evening before the paper was due, I was checking quotes and footnotes when suddenly I saw the trap into which I had fallen. Because of my experience with the Roosevelt paper, I had been blind to Weber's real message. His appeal for a separation of facts from value-judgments was a defense of academic freedom within beleaguered German universities at the beginning of the twentieth century. His plea for a striving toward objectivity in no way ignored the complexity involved, but urged the highest possible standard of professional integrity. Weber's critics, on the other hand, were addressing a community of sociologists currently reaching for respectability as *scientists* in their relatively young field. In order to emphasize the illusions inherent in such a goal, these critics were ignoring the context of Weber's statements and were using them simply as starting points for their arguments.

But once more I had backed myself into a corner. I knew my paper was a thorough exposition of the arguments as the critics had stated them and that it was a good paper. I also knew it would be impossible, given the deadline, to do the whole thing again with any kind of competence. I agonized. Should I submit the paper as it was or do a hurried, inadequate rewrite? I called the professor and told him my problem, asking if I might settle for an incomplete. There was silence for a second and then Dr. Surace told me, "This is one of the rewards in teaching—when students make this kind of discovery on their own." He suggested I leave the paper as it was and simply write an addendum explaining how I had arrived at my change of heart. He said, "It will be the most important part of the paper as far as I am concerned." And so I learned that excellence cannot simply be a product of internal convictions, no matter how passionate they might be. It must not only unearth and account for the facts, it must allow for context—recognizing another time, another place, and other concerns than one's own.

Both experiences were exhilarating—and uncomfortable. Together they taught me that the human mind cannot ever be satisfied with anything less than its own truth. And finding that truth is not simply receiving a product in a single encounter but instead is a process; an ongoing, lifelong struggle against one's own limitations.

I know there are objective standards of excellence developed by discipline and hard work, although these are constantly evolving. I am deeply moved when I encounter excellence in any form—when I listen to Leontyne Price or to a Beethoven symphony, when I see Gelsey Kirkland dance or recognize the grace and will of an Olympic athlete, when I am privileged to contemplate Michelangelo's *Pieta* or the *Winged Victory of Samothrace*—and even when I see an exquisitely sewn dress. My response is reverent. But I believe it is not simply the hard work, the technical perfection, or even the beauty that can bring tears or a stillness in my heart. It is the sense of a purer communication, of being in touch somehow with the deepest and best expression of another human being. Recently Bill and I went to an exhibition of contemporary art. It was one of our most exciting adventures in years. I felt immeasurably privileged to catch glimpses of human spirits through a whole new mode of expression. How strange to appreciate such things without being an artist, even though there may be limits to one's understanding of the specifics of an achievement.

Our eldest son is a mathematician, and one of the sadnesses of my life is that I cannot comprehend the mature expression of *his* creative thinking. Often I have thought how cowardly I was in not taking high school math at junior college so that I might venture classes at UCLA. If I had done so, I might have been able to share at least in a minimal way some of his exciting discoveries. Even without the understanding, though, I am inspired. Seeing excellence in others, despite such barriers speaks to our best self. It puts us in touch with our own essential being and either liberates us vicariously or raises our consciousness of the need to express what is inside.

Subjectively, though, excellence may mean different things to different people. There are those who, mistakenly, I believe, equate excellence with a success that has no concern with means, with the rights or needs of others, in the ruthless pursuit of some external goal. And I find myself searching for greater attributes in those who measure their brand of excellence by money acquired or by position. Without the burden of genius myself, I wonder, too, if the price in abandoned children, betrayed loyalties, and painful loneliness is the only way to reap the Van Goghs and Gauguins that lift my heart. I am glad the judgment is not mine to make.

But for many like me—rejoicing when excellence touches our lives—to hear exhortations toward excellence makes its magic disappear. It becomes another duty, something competing with a host of more immediate demands. Or else we may become cruelly aware of our limitations, fearing that we do not have anything to offer. Mothers dealing with the consuming but limited demands of young children face this kind of dilemma, and it can lead to a feeling of worthlessness no matter how well or how joyfully they may meet those demands. Their children, after all, do not stay young forever. Lowell Bennion has pointed out, "A . . . reason for self-rejection may be the inability of many people in our complex age to find adequate and meaningful ways to express themselves."[1] To urge the pursuit of excellence in such a circumstance only adds to frustration, for it is equated with technical competence. Also, in our highly competitive society, we are conditioned to measure ourselves by comparing what we do with the accomplishments of others. This may serve either to underline our own lack of ability or else give us a smug satisfaction in our own performance. In either event, further effort may be inhibited.

My daughter discovered this in teaching five- and six-year-olds in Primary. Whenever she gave them a common assignment, such as to illustrate something from the lesson, she observed this same pattern emerging. Those who felt inadequate gave up and got into mischief, often demeaning the efforts of those who could do a better job. Others compared and boasted. Always the children compared themselves favorably or unfavorably in the light of what the next person was doing. One week she tried something different. Each child could make something representing a gift that God had given the world. She had a variety of materials from which they could choose, and they each had a different project. One made a tree out of colored paper, another a mountain from some clay, another a snowstorm with cotton balls, another a bird from yellow feathers, and so on. That day each child was totally immersed in the task, pausing only to express excitement about what the next child was doing. They were full of praise for each other's finished products and were united in their pride when they used their works of art in "sharing time" two weeks later.

Each of us is unique. We each have our own view of the world and we each have within us the power, potentially, of expressing that unique awareness. Vincent Van Gogh once observed: "The figure of the labourer—some furrows in a ploughed field—a bit of sand, sea and sky are serious subjects, so difficult, but at the same time so beautiful, that it is indeed worthwhile to devote one's life to the task of expressing the poetry hidden in them."[2] Van Gogh might have added "the poetry *I see* in them," for his sensitive perception was both his gift and his great burden.

Such deep awareness, remaining unexpressed, can become the kind of burden that has been known to cause near-madness in the gifted. But even for the rest of us, with less demanding talent, the lack of opportunity or the inability to find expression for what we feel inside can cause depression or anger, leading perhaps to bitterness and despair or apathy, unless we can hold on to some saving truths.

For me, the first is the bone-deep knowledge that any degree of excellence I achieve will be a by-product of the search for my own truth; it will have to be an honest reflection of whatever I find at any stage in my journey; and the process will be more important than the product. But whoever we are, even the most brilliant among us, and whatever the medium of expression—whether it be gardening, athletics, sewing, dancing, music, painting, or anything else—I believe the process will be important. That process brings us inescapably into the paradox inherent in a Christian life: pursuing the heights of personal excellence while sacrificing self for others. Even more painfully, the paradox requires us, if we love at all, to constantly choose between the needs of loved ones and our own strivings toward self-discovery and development.

Seldom in life are we as free as I was during the hiatus between children and grandchildren, encouraged as I was by a generous-spirited husband. I hope I have described the joy of that liberation. Yet it is the tensions and paradoxes of daily life that force us to choose the values we will live and die by. I think of people I know who choose to set aside their own personal hopes for more fulfilling expression because of the needs of loved ones. Such people often become excellent human beings, but the cost is high. I like to think that the development of their capacities in those other areas is only postponed, not denied. Many can make a single great sacrifice for those they love when the end seems worthwhile. There is a purity and a nobility about such choices. But they also seem easy compared to the insignificant but cumulative demands, constantly consuming time and energy and thinking, that multiply frustration and fragmentation. Our faith, too, can often survive a single dramatic betrayal. Yet the smaller, slowly eroding disillusionments encountered in human society may destroy our trust and inhibit us from sharing who we are with others.

The real challenge is the same for all of us, I believe, differing only in degree, and that is to somehow remain in touch with our own responses to life, to keep alive the uniqueness that shapes those responses, and to accept the refining power of discipline without allowing it to take over our integrity. I learned that vital lesson in ballet school, and I have discovered the same challenge in the Church and in college.

As I think of the wonderful people who have cared about me, I realize how much we need each other on our voyages of self-discovery and development. Without the sensitivity of a mother who first saw a need for expression, a father and sisters who were my friends, a generous husband who has shared my enthusiasm, four children who believed in me, teachers, missionaries, and other friends who have shown genuine interest, I would never have had the courage to share any innermost thoughts.

It is when I remember these people with gratitude that I recognize another important truth. Excellence is not only a by-product, it can also be a means. The times when I am in touch with my deepest spiritual self have been those moments when, for instance, an eleven-year-old girl in Primary trusts me with her problems, or when a young boy pays me the honor of sharing his sense of failure, or when the missionary son of a beloved former missionary friend reveals his aching concerns for those he leads in foreign lands. It is then that I yearn for greater gifts of expression, to mirror back to these honest young people the beauty that I see transcending their pain. At such times—because of such times—I see the real value of excellence, and I find myself longing for the discipline that might help me achieve it.

¹Lowell L. Bennion, "Thou Shalt Love . . . Thyself," *Improvement Era*, April 1962, p. 249.

²*Dear Theo: The Autobiography of Vincent Van Gogh*, edited by Irving Stone (New York: Doubleday & Company, Inc., 1950), p. v.

Irene M. Bates, a native of England, resides in Pacific Palisades, California. She and her husband, William, have four children and nine grandchildren. Sister Bates attended the University of Utah and Santa Monica College and received a bachelor of arts degree in sociology from the University of California at Los Angeles, where she was valedictorian. She has done graduate work in history at Pepperdine University, Malibu. She has published articles in several Church publications and received an award at UCLA for an article on death and dying.

THE TROUBLE WITH EXCELLENCE, OR HOW TO VALUE THE "LESS HONOURABLE" GIFTS

Eugene England

There are some things un-Christlike in much of the world's thinking about and striving for excellence. We talk about "getting ahead," "reaching the top," images that suggest competitive warfare, leaving others behind (or underneath) us, defeated, overwhelmed, perhaps even with broken bodies and souls—*victims* of our excellence. And too often we strivers after excellence are the victims. I know a young mother whose parents and husband have stressed so much her need to excel that she is now immobilized by guilt and fear—guilt that she has never measured up to their expectations and fear that she never will. I've seen my children get so concerned about doing some task excellently in order to live up to high standards set by others, including their parents, that they neglect other important things such as kindness, health, peace of mind— and, ironically, sometimes simply because of that anxiety itself they do poor or incomplete work.

Against these images of competition and the "natural" human strivings and anxieties the images encourage, the scriptures pose very different ideas about excellence. Perhaps the two most sought-after and well-respected badges of excellence in our culture are learning and wealth, but the Book of Mormon prophet Jacob warned us that "the wise, and the learned, and they that are rich, who are puffed up because of their learning, and their wisdom, and their riches—yea, they are they whom [Christ] despiseth; and save they shall cast these things away, and consider themselves fools before

God, and come down in the depths of humility, he will not open unto them." (2 Nephi 9:42.) Four hundred years later, the great King Benjamin's last message to his people was essentially the same: they could not "retain a remission of [their] sins," that is, could not experience the Atonement of Christ and live genuinely moral lives, unless they would "always retain in remembrance, the greatness of God, and [their] own nothingness," their "worthless and fallen state," their awareness that we are "all beggars," dependent on the Lord "for [our] lives and for all that [we] have and are." (Mosiah 4:5, 11, 19-21.)

Christ had his greatest difficulties with the "excellent" and more exalted members of society—the rulers, the scribes and Pharisees, the rich young men. He chose, despite much criticism, to eat with sinners, to take his message and associations mainly to the outcast, the publicans and prostitutes, the poor and unskilled. His apostle Paul expressed explicitly why that was so: "God hath chosen the foolish things of the world to confound the wise; and God hath chosen the weak things of the world to confound the things which are mighty; and base things of the world, and things which are despised, hath God chosen." (1 Corinthians 1:27-28.)

Christ went so far as to identify *himself* as one of these despised and weak and "foolish," one whose own "treasures of wisdom and knowledge" are "hid." (Colossians 2:3.) Again and again he inspired the ancient prophets to prophesy that he would come as Savior not in glory and power nor in forms of excellence that would meet with worldly favor, but as one "despised and rejected of men: a man of sorrows, and acquainted with grief," one whom we would hide our faces from because "we esteemed him not." Contrary to our worldly notions of the proper role of an exalted "messiah," he would bear our grief and carry our sorrows, would be "wounded for our transgressions," "bruised for our iniquities." (See Isaiah 53 and Mosiah 14.) In fact, in remarkable, uniquely insightful visions to Book of Mormon prophets, Christ revealed that his essential mission was to descend below *all* things human so that he could draw all humans to him in the Atonement. He taught Nephi that he would "condescend" or literally *descend with* us into the worst of our earthly experience—that is, in the words he gave King Benjamin, into "temptations, and pain of body, hunger, thirst, and fatigue, even more than man can suffer." And to Alma he made clear that he would actually "take upon him the pains and the sicknesses of his people," would "take upon him their infirmities, that his bowels may be filled with mercy, according to the flesh, that he may know according to the flesh how to succor his people according to their infirmities." (See 1 Nephi 11:13-27; Mosiah 3:5-7; Alma 7: 11-13.)

   Christ teaches that it was necessary for him literally to take on himself our human sicknesses and infirmities, to become, in the world's eyes, meek and lowly, weak and foolish. Moreover, we must *see* him as such, as "the least of these, my brethren," if we are to be able to overcome our worldly pride, accept ourselves as loved by him despite our own weaknesses and sins, and thus be able to experience "at onement" with him and be saved. If we cannot accept ourselves and others as infinitely valuable, despite our infirmities and failures, if we cannot feel the energizing joy of Paul, who exclaimed as his central, redeeming insight, "While we were yet sinners, Christ died for us" (Romans 5:8), then our own religious and moral life will be incapacitated. The central effort of Christ's at onement is to draw us to him by moving us, with his infinite suffering in the garden where he achieved complete identification with us through the "bowels of mercy," to accept ourselves unconditionally, as he has accepted us, and thus find means that we "may have faith unto repentance." (Alma 34:13-15.)

   But hold on, you might well say: if striving for excellence is so dangerous and humility paramount, what about all the emphasis in the scriptures on seeking the best gifts, on "being perfect" ourselves "even as [God] is perfect"? What about Joseph Smith's constant striving and his witness that all who come into the world "are capable of enlargement"— and Brigham Young's continual emphasis on "eternal progression"? Why did Elder Neal A. Maxwell write an invigorating book on "a more excellent way" and President

Spencer W. Kimball energize the Church with a call to "lengthen our stride"? And why, for heaven's sake, are you now offering us a whole volume of essays encouraging "excellence"?

The answer to those good questions is simply that we are dealing here with a paradox, one captured best in the words of Christ: "Whosoever shall seek to save his life shall lose it: and whosoever shall lose his life shall preserve it." (Luke 17:33.) Excellence vs. humility, striving to save our lives vs. finding them through giving, winning the "race" for ourselves vs. sacrificing all for others—these are indeed "contraries," horns of a dilemma, poles of a paradox. But they are unavoidable parts of a real universe in which there must needs be "opposition in all things" (2 Nephi 2:11), and where we can best learn how to live by thinking through the opposed values and reaching some new, transcendent way of living that preserves them both, despite the conflict. As Joseph Smith wrote, "'By proving contraries,' truth is made manifest." (*History of the Church* 6:428.)

The Lord has given us the help necessary to think through these particular contraries in two great parallel passages of scripture about gifts, Doctrine and Covenants 46 and 1 Corinthians 12. In that wonderful invitation to the Latter-day Saints of 1831 to learn to appreciate each other, themselves, and all his Father's children, Christ first taught the new church "never to cast any one out from your public meetings" nor to exclude from church meetings anyone who is "earnestly seeking after the kingdom." He goes on, in that spirit, to teach these new converts, very anxious to progress and prove themselves and (apparently) to judge those who seemed less valiant, that though "all have not every gift given unto them," to "every man is given a gift by the Spirit of God." (D&C 46:3, 5, 11.) To make this perfectly clear Christ enumerates many of the gifts, emphasizing that each is different from the other but that *all are equally valuable* and *acceptable:* faith to know that Jesus Christ is the Son of God and faith to believe on the words of those who know; differences of administration (leadership) and diversities of operations (practical skills); wisdom (theoretical) and knowledge (factual); faith to be healed and faith to heal; working of miracles and prophetic insight; speaking in tongues and interpreting what those speakers say.

In this revelation, Christ continually repeats a central message that could help us all learn to strive for excellence unselfishly, to avoid losing our lives through seeking to save them: The gifts are given, with at least one provided each person, not as a reward or a special blessing to that person, not as a reason for pride or sense of special privilege, but "that all may be profited thereby" (v. 12), "that the manifestations of the Spirit may be given to every man to profit withal" (v. 16). As a solution to the danger of pride and self-centeredness, Christ admonishes the young Church—and all of us—that we should "always remember, and always retain in [our] minds what those gifts are" (v. 10) and "give thanks unto God in the Spirit for *whatsoever* blessing [we] are blessed with" (v. 32; italics added).

This revelation repeats in shortened form what Christ had already taught the apostle Paul eighteen hundred years before. In his first letter to the Corinthians, Paul enumerates the same gifts and also emphasizes that these differences in the members of the body of Christ have nothing to do with the relative value of each member—*all* are needed: "If the whole body were an eye, where were the hearing? If the whole were hearing, where were the smelling? But now hath God set the members every one of them in the body, as it hath pleased him." (1 Corinthians 12:17-18.) But Paul carries the point to an unusual insight, which Christ can assume we have in mind when we read the shorter version in Doctrine and Covenants 46: "Nay, much more those members of the body, which seem to be more feeble, are necessary: and those members of the body, which we think to be less honourable, upon these we bestow more abundant honour; and our uncomely parts have more abundant comeliness." (1 Corinthians 12:22-23.)

This is strange doctrine, of the kind Paul knew would be "foolishness to the Greeks"—that is, to the rational, worldly mind. What? We should honor *more* the feeble, the uncomely among us? Scandalous! But Paul has a good reason for telling us to do precisely that—*if* we can see the matter from God's perspective, which is not concerned with comparative, individual excellence but with helping *all* his children become like him and also helping those children learn how to *help each other* reach that goal. This is Paul's reason: "Our comely parts have no need: but God hath tempered the body together, having given more abundant honour to that part which lacked: that there should be no schism in the body; but that the members should have the same care one for another. And whether one member suffer, all the members suffer with it; or one member be honoured, all the members rejoice with it." (1 Corinthians 12:24-26.) The "comely gifts"—such as knowledge and wealth—will normally get much honor in human society, in fact, usually so much that Christ has to warn us to give them away, share them completely, or they will canker our souls and destroy us rather than being a blessing to us and others. On the other hand, we must seek to see each other's gifts, however feeble or uncomely in the world's eyes. We must learn to suffer together and share honor together so that we can all be blessed by all our diverse gifts. That mutual blessing, in fact, is why God gave the gifts in the first place.

I know a woman who has great gifts of the less comely kind, and I had to be helped a great deal by the Lord to see them. I first knew her when she approached me for help after hearing me talk in her ward about the grace of Christ, his unconditional love for sinners. How could she cope with her struggles and feelings concerning the two-year-old son she held, a spastic quadriplegic, apparently blind and deaf from some kind of neglect in the hospital after birth? Why had the Lord allowed this to happen to one son and not its twin? Why had priesthood blessings that seemed to promise recovery not yet been fulfilled? How could she and her husband go on holding the boy nearly twenty-four hours a day to keep him from choking to death? How could she be forgiven for sometimes wanting him dead? I didn't have answers, but I held her son while she enjoyed a quiet hour in Sunday School with her husband, and I offered help from my family so she and her husband could get away for some time together to repair their marriage, which she admitted had suffered much from the strains.

Almost a year later I was called to be bishop of the ward where this woman lived, and as I prayed about the initial organization, I was directed to call her as my first Relief Society president. It made no sense. She was still greatly burdened. She and her husband had decided not to sue the hospital, because "with the Lord's help we are making it, and the suit would waste much money and hurt people to no good purpose," but the husband had left business school to cope with the enormous financial burdens and was planning to move the family to Salt Lake City. However, the call was clear and they accepted. Then I began to learn why.

The gifts she had been given and developed while enduring this great trial came to the fore as she visited each ward family, opened herself and her life entirely to her sisters, and conducted her interviews, her meetings, and even her casual conversations with absolute honesty and down-to-earth forthrightness. Her husband had begun to learn the same forthrightness. He took his painfully abnormal-looking son before the congregation during our first testimony meeting and introduced him to the ward as one whom the Lord loved, who needed *their* love and unself-conscious attention, and whose parents needed their help. I assigned a couple each Sunday to help them through church with their son. And as the members of our ward (mainly bright, upwardly mobile young pre-professionals) experienced quite directly the struggles, the ups and downs of anguish and hope, the need for help, and the enduring through which this family lived each day, we all found how much more those members of the body, which seem to be more feeble, are necessary.

I know of a young family in which both parents are seriously handicapped in mental ability and social training. A large part of the energy and resources of their ward go to helping that couple and their bright, energetic child survive and stay together as a family, but the bishop feels that the Lord directed the couple to his ward and that they constitute one of the ward's great blessings. Others in the ward are sometimes, with good reason, offended by this couple—by their insensitive intrusions into their homes or into the decorum of the sacrament meetings and classes (where I understand they sometimes give "inconsequential" and lengthy testimonies or comments), by their noisy but inadequate attempts to discipline their child, by their lack of training in personal cleanliness, in housekeeping, and in finances, all of which leave them constantly in trouble and troubling to others. But I'm told that even the offended ones are learning some surprising lessons. One recently phoned the bishop to confess in tears that she had learned, through trying to help and be a friend to someone so difficult, what charity really was—how hard and important it was—and had herself embarked on some difficult repentance as a result. Others have grown in the essentials of Church service more than ever before, through taking on total responsibility for training the man in financial matters, even in getting and keeping a job, or working with the couple to establish a family schedule, or helping the woman learn how to manage a home for the first time and how to help the child with learning and discipline. Now, as the couple have progressed to a steady income and stable family life, with a strong, continuing support system firmly around them, the man has been given the Melchizedek Priesthood and the whole ward is looking forward, with unusual understanding of tough service and the grace of God, to the couple's going to the temple to be sealed for eternity. And that is part of that couple's gift to the ward, their feeble gift, their very unusual "excellence" that blesses all.

Most of us have known people with such feeble, less comely, and therefore less honored—or even unrecognized—gifts. My neighbor, Roman Andrus, is a fine artist who has trained generations of students and painted some honored portraits and landscapes, but he has a less honored gift that is very important to his neighbors and ward: the gift of telling stories from his youth that convey integrity and humor and love of life. He has probably done more for the salvation of myself and people I love with those excellent stories than with all his excellent paintings. I have another neighbor who has cared for her totally immobilized husband for many years and whose great gift, of great value to all who know her, is unromantic, gritty, spirited endurance. Her husband's gift is vulnerable need, the courage to keep reading and thinking and reciting poetry and talking through all the pain of bedsores and the humiliation and exposure as we carry and shift and feed and bathe him.

You know the class member who always has the needed facts, even though she can't interpret them well, and the one who is a great interpreter, even though he is impervious to being confused by facts—and how *both* are needed for a good class. Or the mother of six who always seems to know when someone needs help—and who helps that person without anyone else knowing. I know one such woman who always has two or three "lost" people, young and old, living at her home. She is able to hear some guardian angel whisper to her that a young widow in the ward needs a thousand dollars to survive just a little longer, or that a young couple across town, unable to have their own children and unable to adopt because of a huge hospital debt, need a loan so they can go ahead with a family. Excellence for her is not "getting ahead" or "on top," it is not competition and struggle; rather, it is a simple expression of what she is because of the Lord's "less honourable" gifts to her, by which he blesses many others. And my children are learning to be like her.

In a recent address as president of the Association for Mormon Letters, Lavina Fielding Anderson told how she had learned, from a testimony at a gathering of Mormon women in Nauvoo, that even these feeble gifts, even our weaknesses and vulnerabilities, are what we consecrate to the Lord in the temple to use as he will—and that use might include talking about them in *our* writing and testimonies:

"Catherine Stokes, a black convert in a Chicago ward, related the experience of going to the temple for the first time. 'I took my blackness with me,' she said, 'and that was part of what I consecrated.' She told of the woman who assisted her in the initiatory ordinance, barely able to articulate through her tears, and apologizing at the end because she had not wanted her personal emotions to interfere with Cathy's experience. 'But I've never had the privilege of doing this for a black woman before,' she explained, 'and I'm so grateful.' Cathy reassured her, 'That's all right. That's one of the things I can do for *you* that no one else in the temple today could do.' As she summed up the experience, she added, 'My blackness is one of the things that the Lord can use if he wants to'—and apparently it has been a most successful collaboration."

Excellence, it seems, is not such a simple matter as we might have supposed. It is deadly dangerous as a goal if it leads to destructive competition with others and to pride—or even to mere self-preoccupation, a focus on *our* progress and salvation. In fact, our concern for excellence can destroy excellence. It is often not truly seen, in others and ourselves, because we are beguiled by the honors of men and neglect the excellent but feeble and less comely gifts God has given us, those on which we must "bestow more abundant honour." Excellence sometimes, made into a primary goal, sought after directly, leads us to lose our earthly life—in anguish and depression at our failures—and to forfeit our eternal redemption because we cannot experience the Atonement until we accept God's love of us as we are.

President Spencer W. Kimall, though in many ways our most energetic and motivating recent prophet, has also given us good guidelines and example to counteract these misunderstandings of excellence. He fully revealed the paradox by insisting that his biography, *Spencer W. Kimball*, include, with all the record of achievements, the passages from his personal journals that record his own doubts and despair, his conviction that he was failing his calling, could never measure up. Among a litany of expressions of inadequacy, we see especially the poignancy of his many illnesses—boils, heart trouble, cancer—that caught him up in a vicious circle of feeling "guilty for failing to carry his share of the load," convinced that he was "the least" of the apostles, that the others were "smoother, smarter, more efficient, better educated," and that he must work *harder*, even at the danger of ruining his health, to compensate. "Thousands of people in the Church are measuring the Church, their Church, by me," he wrote. "They look at me with my smallness, my ineptitudes, my weaknesses, my narrow limitations and say,

'What a weak Church to have such weak leadership.' It is one of the things that has brought me to my back now. I have tried by double expenditure of energy to measure up." (Edward L. Kimball and Andrew E. Kimball, Jr., *Spencer W. Kimball,* Bookcraft, 1977, p. 253.)

President Kimball risked death by asking the doctors, in their operation to remove throat cancer, to leave part of his larynx so he could learn the very difficult way of talking that would then still be possible and continue to serve with that "weak" voice, the small but piercing voice that has continued for over twenty-five years to make him possibly our finest, certainly our most challenging and energizing, Mormon orator of the twentieth century. Every time we hear that soft, rough, unique voice we should remember what he has paid for it and remember that excellence in speaking is not winning speech contests or developing a polished and resonant radio announcer's style, but clear sense of purpose and courage to risk letting the Lord use us, even in our weakness. And it is also humility, as President Kimball reminds us constantly with his self-deprecating manner. For instance, when he stated at the close of the October 1975 general conference that his life could be improved and that he intended to do so by applying the ideas from his brethren he had jotted down during the conference, we were moved to increased trust and desire to follow his example rather than any lack of confidence. We all need to be as open about our opinions, our convictions, our experiences and mistakes, even our shortcomings. They are among our gifts—to be used and thus made into strengths, made excellent.

President Brigham Young, who was the prophet of the nineteenth century perhaps most like Spencer Kimball in his energetic, practical counsel and humble forthrightness, gave what seems to me the best help in resolving the paradox of excellence versus humility. He recognized that the desire for excellence—what he called "the principle of improvement, . . . of increase, of exaltation"—is "the main spring of all action" and "should be understood by the child and the adult." (*Journal of Discourses* 2:91.) However, he also taught that not only do we each have a different gift but we each can become perfect in our own small sphere of effort and influence with that gift—and then be given more and greater gifts and constantly move on to perfection in those higher spheres. Thus, without feeling we are caught up in competition with others, or depressed by a sense of failure because we are never perfect in some absolute sense, compared to others and our own eventual possibilities, we can do the best we can day by day with our most feeble and unhonored gifts, even our weaknesses and needs, letting others also be blessed by blessing us. We can see Christ in the least of our brethren, in the weak and needy around us, even the sick and captive and sinning—even in ourselves. We can be moved to accept ourselves as acceptable to Christ, even though we have failed him, and thus we can receive the Atonement and renew it constantly through the sacrament and temple ordinances and by daily enduring to the end. This is how Brigham Young understood the process by which *every one* of us can find our own unique mode of excellence and aspire, with all others, to Godhood:

"We can still improve, we are made for that purpose, our capacities are organized to expand until we can receive into our comprehension celestial knowledge and wisdom, and to continue worlds without end. . . . If men can understand and receive it, mankind are organized to receive intelligence until they become perfect in the sphere they are appointed to fill, which is far ahead of us at present. When we use the term perfection, it applies to man in his present condition, as well as to heavenly beings. We are now, or may be as perfect in *our sphere* as God and Angels are in theirs, but the greatest intelligence in existence can continually ascend to greater heights of perfection. . . . It is the Deity within us that causes increase." (JD 1:92-93.)

Our paradox has turned into many "contraries" concerning excellence, and all of them can be helpful if we will follow Joseph Smith's lead and "prove" or test them out. Striving for excellence will destroy us and others if it prevents us from accepting and loving ourselves and others *as we are now.* Excellence as a goal defined in worldly images can blind us to the destructive effects of competing with others and make us ignore the "less honourable" but in many ways more needed gifts of humility, peacemaking, comfort-giving, humor, vulnerability, need for help, and so forth, gifts that we need to recognize and honor more—and develop in ourselves and others—so that such gifts can themselves become excellent and a blessing to all: "Brethren, if a man be overtaken in a fault, ye which are spiritual, restore such an one in the spirit of meekness; considering thyself, lest thou also be tempted. Bear ye one another's burdens, and so fulfil the law of Christ. For if a man think himself to be somebody, when he is nothing, he deceiveth himself." (Galatians 6: 1-3.) And the final paradox, as Paul taught us in his discussion on gifts, as a lead-in to his great sermon on the nature of unconditional love, is that though we must each strive to be excellent in our own gifts, the *greatest of all excellences* is to care most about helping others become excellent in *their* gifts. "Covet earnestly the best gifts," he declared, "and yet shew I unto you a more excellent way. Though I speak with the tongues of men and angels, . . . and understand all mysteries, and all knowledge; and though I have all faith, . . . and have not charity, I am nothing." (1 Corinthians 12:31– 13:1-2.)

Eugene England and his wife, Charlotte, have six children. She helps him in his assignments as professor of English at Brigham Young University and bishop of the BYU 139th Ward, and he helps her in her dollmaking profession and in developing an ice cream parlor in Provo. Dr. England writes poetry, personal essays (collected and published in <u>Dialogues with Myself</u>), biography (<u>Brother Brigham</u>), and criticism of American—and especially Mormon—literature. He is currently at work on a book to be titled <u>Shakespeare and Melville: Man's Final Lore</u>, and a biography of Joseph Smith, <u>You Never Knew My Heart</u>.

TWO CHEERS FOR EXCELLENCE

Bruce C. Hafen

I am not very enthusiastic about lectures and books on "success" and "excellence" among the Latter-day Saints.

I do agree fervently with Elder Richard L. Evans, who once told a small Church audience in which I sat, "It is good to be faithful. But how much better it is to be faithful and competent." I share this conviction to the extent of doubting that one is truly faithful if he is less competent than he could be. I know firsthand how the Brethren feel about the quality of what is done in the Church Educational System. For instance, I have felt the intense concern of President Marion G. Romney about the professional quality of the J. Reuben Clark Law School at Brigham Young University. For President Romney, questions by law students about a choice between spiritual excellence and intellectual excellence make no sense at all. Of course spiritual excellence comes first; but to him, as to his great mentor, J. Reuben Clark, intellectual excellence is simply part of abundant spiritual excellence, and religious devotion is not an acceptable excuse for professional mediocrity.

Yet I feel an ever-deepening uneasiness about our uncritically accepting the assumptions of the Yankee ethic of success, which can be so competitive, self-centered, and superficial. That is why I have only two cheers for excellence. I have reservations not because I believe it justifiable for us to exert less than our finest efforts; rather, I fear that without a wise perspective, an unqualified commitment to goals and excellence can distort our understanding of certain long-term principles about life and its larger purposes—even if we do put forth great effort.

Consider some examples:

I recently talked with a young woman who had unselfishly worked very hard at being a good wife and mother through several difficult years of marriage. But now the marriage was breaking down. Her husband had developed emotional problems that seriously threatened the spiritual (and at times even the physical) survival of the woman and her children. Surrounded by many questions, she asked the one that haunted her most: "How could this have happened, when I have tried so hard to do everything the Church has taught me to do?"

Then I talked with a man who had recently joined the Church and found shortly after his conversion that he had a terminal illness. He too had done everything within his power to live as he should, making many sacrifices because of his wholehearted acceptance of the gospel. With his newfound hopes for life now cut so bluntly short, he could not make sense of it. He wondered aloud, "What have I done wrong?"

One day a young father who had a learning disability and little education asked me a question that he said had worried him for years: "Do you have to be smart and have a good education to get into the celestial kingdom?" I knew him to be a genuine, decent, and hardworking person. He had never tasted of success the way most people measure it and probably never would. As he waited for my answer, I noticed the tears beginning to fill his eyes.

To these people, the high-sounding goal of "excellence" is not so much a source of motivation as it is a source of frustration and discouragement. They have worked as hard as their circumstances allowed, but the rewards they thought were supposed to accompany great effort have somehow eluded them. Not only were they confused about not being rewarded; their failure to achieve had produced feelings of total personal failure.

At a more general level, from the time we are schoolchildren, we grow up with grading curves of one kind or another. Because curves by definition have many more losers than winners, most people develop a sense of basic inferiority. Most of us aren't among the top ten percent of anything. Our disappointments range from being the last chosen in a sandlot game to seeing our income range officially designated as "lower middle class," to seeing somebody else always chosen as mother of the year.

Yet something fascinates the American public with being Number One. Hugh Nibley has noted that many of us would rather be Number One in hell than a doorkeeper in the house of the Lord. Or, as Satan put it in Milton's *Paradise Lost,* "To reign is worth ambition . . . / Better to reign in hell than to serve in heav'n."

The competitive environment is all around us. For instance, my younger children have always confused the state and national top-ten rankings among teams in high schools, colleges, and the pros. But they've picked up the central message: if you're not ranked, you must not count for much. So when our sixth-grader's basketball team completed its city league schedule without winning a game, all our well-meant advice about the value of learning to play the game fell on deaf and droopy ears. I was reminded of the poem a depressed junior high student wrote after his team got trounced in the district tournament, and certain players' parents made it clear what incompetent wretches the team members were. Said his last line, in a mildly cynical turn of Grantland Rice's old phrase, "They cared not how we played the game, but if we won or lost."

So I cannot help wondering what we are doing to each other in the Church these days, as we subtly but continually reinforce in one another the assumption that tangible and visible "rewards" and "success" are promised those who do what is right or even those who work their hardest. Where does that assumption come from? It certainly is not taught by the gospel. On the contrary, the gospel of Jesus Christ teaches that the lone and dreary world of mortality is soaked through with adversity and trouble—not to torture us, but to teach us. "In sorrow thou shalt bring forth children," Eve was told. And to Adam the Lord said, "Cursed is the ground *for thy sake;* in sorrow shalt thou eat of it all the days of thy life. . . . In the sweat of thy face shalt thou eat bread, till thou return unto the ground." (Genesis 3:16-19. Italics added.) If Adam and Eve had never left that idyllic garden, "They would have remained in a state of innocence, having no joy, for they knew no misery." (2 Nephi 2:23.) It was intended from the beginning, "in the wisdom of him who knoweth all things," (2 Nephi 2:24), that we should "taste the bitter," for the express purpose that we "may know to prize the good" (Moses 6:55).

The gospel promises rewards, but "not as the world giveth." (John 14:27.) Rather, "he who doeth the works of righteousness shall receive his reward, even peace in this world, and eternal life in the world to come." (D&C 59:23.) By contrast, those whose vision is limited to this world measure their success only by being seen of men. Of such the Savior said, "They have their reward." (Matthew 6:5.)

Despite these plain teachings, the assumptions of contemporary America's success ethic are deeply and powerfully ingrained in many members of the Church. This may be partly the influence of history, since our acceptance of these attitudes has relatively recent origins.

During the first sixty or seventy years after the organization of the Church, there were profound distinctions between the culture of the Latter-day Saints and the culture of America. The Saints had their own ideas, not only about theology, but also about the total cultural environment, including economic, social, and political systems. During the nineteenth-century heyday of Yankee individualism, "survival of the fittest" was in all its brutality a cherished way of American life. But in the mountain lands of the West, the Great Basin Kingdom of that era was as isolated culturally as it was geographically. Indeed, the Church and its people had been rejected by the melting pot called America in large measure because they would not melt into the pattern of Yankee values. Economically, the Saints sought a deliberate isolation, stressing cooperation among themselves while rejecting the nation's every-man-for-himself brand of free enterprise. Politically, both the City of Joseph Smith

(Nauvoo) and the Great Basin of Brigham Young sought a harmony between religious and political life that was never understood by outsiders. Socially, the practice of polygamy became the last straw to a noncomprehending American nation, though it only symbolized a far more fundamental misunderstanding.

After being pushed to the brink of destruction in a story too long to recount here, the Saints ultimately embraced their fellow Americans and worked very hard after the turn of the century to dispel former impressions of their excessive peculiarity. During the twentieth century, the Church and its members became increasingly accepted as a legitimate part of "Main Street, U.S.A." Members of the Church are today considered among the most ardent defenders of success-oriented entrepreneurial values, as evidenced by the widespread belief that Utah is among the nation's most promising markets for get-rich-quick artists.

In some sense, the apparent assimilation of American Latter-day Saints into the materialistic society of twentieth-century America parallels the assimilation of ancient Israel following its captivity into Babylonian culture. At first the Jewish captives longed to return home to the land and ways of their fathers. But after a time they had become sufficiently integrated into the larger culture that when the opportunity finally came to return home, most preferred to stay. As observed by the Jewish historian, Ernest Renan: "Many of the Israelites . . . found themselves very comfortable in Babylonia. Thanks to their practical dexterity, they were able to find a thousand ways of amassing a fortune in a city devoted to luxury and pleasure. . . . They were not at all tempted to . . . return to a narrow strip of land condemned . . . to remain eternally poor."[1] Perhaps similar feelings might be experienced by some Latter-day Saints today who may already be so attached to the ways of modern Babylon that they could be unwilling to leave it, either literally or figuratively.

The competitive ethic of personal success and achievement is one of the chief characteristics of U.S. culture. It is not, therefore, surprising that this set of values would creep into the contemporary attitudes of Latter-day Saints through their embracing of Yankee traditions in the twentieth century. For that reason, it is worth a brief glance at the origins of the success ethic in the building of the American character, so we know what the ethic is, where it came from, and perhaps what is wrong with it.

The American tradition of worshipping at the altar of excellence is as current as the latest poll in football teams or hit recordings, and as old as the ancient Greeks, whose values America inherited through the European Renaissance: "The central ethical idea in Homer can be found in the instructions that the father of Achilles gives to his son when he sends him off to fight at Troy: 'Always be the best and distinguished above others.'"[2]

The more recent basic source of this competitive heritage is Puritanism—the Puritan ethic—thought by many historians to have fueled much of the achievement and the rugged individualism of American history. According to the Calvinist theology on which Puritan thought was based, "the elect" of God were chosen totally by predestined divine grace, while all other people remained totally depraved. Because of the anti-authoritarianism that ran through Calvin's teachings, it was not the place of the clergy, civil authorities, or any other human being to judge who had been selected by God's will for salvation. Thus, one could feel within his own heart that he had been chosen if he saw the fruits of God's grace in his personal affairs—that is, if he were "successful." Such outward evidence also had a way of convincing others of one's divine election. In this way, ideas of religious predestination that seemed to deny free will had the paradoxical effect of creating "a more powerful stimulus to extreme effort and a more moral force than any doctrine of human freedom."[3] In this way, "instead of turning to fatalism and resignation," the Puritan ethic "became a challenge to unrelenting effort, a sense of burning conviction, a conviction of having a mission, of . . . being on the side of that Almighty Power which must in the end be everlastingly triumphant."[4]

One other component that emerged in the nineteenth-century doctrines of Yankee self-interest was social Darwinism, the idea that under Nature's laws for developing superior characteristics in a species, the triumphs of the strong are supposed to emerge amid the disasters of the weak. As described by John D. Rockefeller, one of the presumably successful products of this process, "The American Beauty rose, with all its splendor and fragrance, could not have been produced without sacrificing the buds that grew up around it." In a similar way, the development of a large business that displaces its competition is "merely survival of the fittest . . . the working-out of a law of nature and a law of God."[5]

But there is something wrong with these ideas. A belief in "survival of the fittest" seems to justify the essentially un-Christian idea of putting others down to pull ourselves up. In contrast, the Lord has said: "He that exalteth himself shall be abased, and he that abaseth himself shall be exalted." (D&C 101:42.)

The Calvinist doctrines that underlie the Puritan ethic are even more misleading. Not only does Calvinism deny free agency; it also teaches that our successes are evidence that God has chosen us, while our failures are evidence that God has rejected us. This logic seems compelling enough that those who believe it are more likely to seek success than they are to seek God. At the other extreme, those who experience personal failures can all too easily assume they are the rejects of heaven. When self-doubt of that kind sets in, the will to keep striving may wane. How natural it is to assume, when we don't appear to be doing "excellently," that the perfection process is not working. But the exact opposite may be true: our moments of greatest stress and difficulty are often the times when the refiner's fire is doing its most purifying work.

During his dark days in Liberty Jail, Joseph Smith was so discouraged that he cried out, "O God, where art thou? And where is the pavilion that covereth thy hiding place?" (D&C 121:1.) But the Lord's voice whispered to him, "Know thou, my son, that all these things shall give thee experience, and shall be for thy good." (D&C 122:7.) The Savior himself reached such an extreme and lonely agony on the cross that he pled aloud, "My God, my God, why hast thou forsaken me?" (Matthew 27:46.) Yet this depth of darkness was his hour of greatest triumph.

In the stirring story of Job in the Old Testament, Satan, Job's friends, and Job's wife all seemed to believe in some variation on the theme of the Puritan ethic. Satan claimed at the beginning of the story that the only reason for Job's obedience was that God had blessed him with such prosperity. Who wouldn't fear God, he suggested, when doing so obviously advances one's materialistic self-interest? In response, God sent adversity to Job, with a fury that appeared at best unfair. It certainly seemed unfair to Job's wife, whose assumption that God had rejected them was matched by her assumption that their only alternative was to reject God: "Then said his wife unto him, Dost thou still retain thine integrity? curse God, and die." (Job 2:9.)

Job's friends took the view that anybody with Job's problems must obviously have brought them upon himself by unrighteousness. "Who ever perished, being innocent?" (Job 4:7.) So they urged him to repent of whatever he was doing to anger God, promising an immediate return to prosperity as the reward: "If thou return to the Almighty, thou shalt be built up. . . . Yea, the Almighty shall be thy defense, and thou shalt have plenty of silver." (Job 22:23, 25.) But Job had the insight they lacked about the nature of both God's love and the mortal experience: "If I have made gold my hope, . . . this also were an iniquity." (Job 31:24, 28.) Job understood that the only reliable constant in life is our relationship with God, with whatever combination of joy and affliction may be ours in that relationship: "The Lord gave, and the Lord hath taken away; blessed be the name of the Lord." (Job 1:21.) "Till I die I will not remove mine integrity from me. . . . For what is the hope of the hypocrite, though he hath gained, when God taketh away his soul? Will God hear his cry when trouble cometh upon him? Will he delight himself in the Almighty? will he always call upon God? . . . But where shall wisdom be found? and where is the place of understanding? Man knoweth not the price thereof. . . . It cannot be gotten for gold. . . . Behold, the fear of the Lord, that is wisdom; and to depart from evil is understanding." (Job 27:5, 8-10; 28:12-14, 28.)

I am addressing primarily a need for perspective. I do not mean to diminish the value of serious commitments to personal achievement and responsibility. The willingness to strive and keep striving is at the heart of Job's message to us. But the striving must be to find God and to accept fully the experiences he knows will enlarge our souls. The trouble with modern pursuits of excellence is that they can become a striving to please other men, or at least to impress them or to seek their approval. A desire for such approval is not all bad, especially among Church members, who generally reserve their approval for accomplishments having positive value. But man is not finally our judge, and making too much of either the affirmative or the adverse judgments of others can actually undermine our relationship with God and our development of sound values.

There are many ways in which our natural desire for the approval and praise of other people can distort our perspective. For example, today's society gives great prominence to financial success and public visibility. However, as stated by Elder Boyd K. Packer: "It is the misapprehension of most people that if you are good, really good, at what you do, you will eventually be both widely known and well compensated. . . . The world seems to work on that premise. The premise is false. It is not true. The Lord taught otherwise. . . . You need not be either rich or hold high position to be completely successful and truly happy. . . . We want our children and their children to know that the choice of life is not between fame and obscurity, nor is the choice between wealth and poverty. The choice is between good and evil, and that is a very different matter indeed."[6]

Joseph F. Smith, the sixth president of the Church, once expressed the same attitude, saying that true greatness is "to do well those things which God ordained to be the common lot of man-kind."[7]

But as our society has become more materialistic, our

vision has been blurred on many issues of meaning and value. One of the tragedies of the extreme version of today's feminist movement, for example, has been the growing public attitude that unless society places some tangible economic value on female labor, the labor is of questionable worth. One result of this assumption is that women (and men) increasingly believe they should measure life's satisfactions in terms of professional or other career accomplishments. This premise has found its way into virtually every corner of public discourse these days, even while reliable empirical studies affirm that successful professional men still regard their families as a greater source of personal satisfaction than their careers.[8] Moreover, 90 percent of American workers find more purpose in their leisure time activities than in their work.[9]

The effect of emphasizing "individual gain" on our view of women was captured by Brigham Young University anthropologist Merlin Myers: "Members of society are important, not in terms of their kinship relations, but rather in terms of their success in getting gain. . . . For us, gain—most often reckoned in monetary terms—is the measure of social worth and status. The begetting, bearing and caring for children does not produce gain in the currently accepted sense of the word. Rather, [childrearing] may put strain on what gain is available, or may impede the freedom and mobility of a person in his or her quest for gain. Women are thus caught in the very unenviable position of having the most decisive attributes of their femininity, or womanhood, denigrated by the society in which they live as being an obstacle to their achieving worth. . . . Day-care centers and old people's homes . . . free those who would be responsible for children and parents in societies where kinship norms prevail, to pursue personal gain in one form or another. . . . (Compare this with the statement of the heart-rent Rachel to her husband, Jacob, 'Give me children, else I die'!)"[10]

Another distortion in our thinking about personal achievement is our inability to see that many forms of apparent success and apparent failure result from causes beyond our control. For that reason, it is not always fair to impute responsibility for Triumph or Disaster to those who seem to have found them. (Rudyard Kipling's "If" expresses the hope that we may "meet with Triumph and Disaster and treat those two impostors just the same.") During my experience as a practicing lawyer, I encountered many people whose business success was more the result of good guesses, good connections, and favorable market conditions than the result of great attributes of personal character or even good management. On the other hand, I knew a number of fine people who appeared to fail temporarily because of business conditions or other forces quite beyond their control.

I have made similar observation on college campuses. A common problem among students is lack of self-esteem. Many reasons for their low morale are readily apparent: not having a nice car—or not having a car at all; not having lots of friends or nice clothes or a big scholarship; not enjoying a position of prominence in campus life; feeling socially unsuccessful or intellectually inferior; feeling too poor or too plain in appearance. It is also common among students on large campuses to simply feel discouraged and overwhelmed by the daily process of being graded (as if in some eternal sense) by relentless examinations, papers, and grading curves. Many of the obstacles to success in the campus environment, as elsewhere, are from sources beyond the control of the student, whether that is one's native intelligence, looks, or family wealth. The most frustrating feelings, not only about one's belief in oneself but also about one's belief in the fairness of life, come from the hopelessness of trying to control forces that are simply beyond our reach.

Reinhold Neibuhr's oft-quoted advice is worth pondering: "God, give us the serenity to accept what cannot be changed, courage to change what should be changed, and the wisdom to distinguish the one from the other."

From God's perspective on our lives, we can control the things that really matter: the righteousness of our desires, the purity of our motives, the wholeheartedness of our efforts to love God and keep his commandments, the genuineness of our interest in other people, and the extent to which our efforts reflect our inborn capacity. Indeed, I think that one way to distinguish what matters a great deal from what does not matter so much is to ask whether the subject is within our control. If it is, then it probably matters enough to merit our attention. But if the subject of our fretting is inherently beyond our control, it is not likely that God will hold us responsible for our ultimate success or failure as to that concern.

Our perspective can also be impaired by assuming that achievement in one area of endeavor establishes some general level of merit or worth. However, no specialized success can compensate for weakness of character. Moreover, all people represent some combination of strengths and limitations. As Richard L. Evans once said, "Nobody has everything that everyone else has." As a young teenager, I didn't understand that. I somehow got the idea that all people were ranked along some vertical scale from really being somebody to not counting for much. I gradually came to understand, as I came to know the private lives of more people over time, that each of us has been given some spiritual gift that is uniquely our own. ("To every man is given a gift by the Spirit of God," D&C 46:11.) Further, each of us has weaknesses and limitations that are sufficient to keep us modest. As the Lord told Moroni, "I give unto men weakness that they may be humble." (Ether 12:27.) Each person represents some particular combination of gifts and limitations as we stand on a horizontal plane with one another. But the heroes of public attention are shown to us by the media as if they were superhuman in every respect.

Finally, our preoccupation with achievement as man defines it focuses our attention on man, rather than God, as our judge. However, not only is popular opinion too fickle and fleeting to serve as a reliable guide of our self-worth; others cannot possibly know enough about our hearts and the innermost elements of our lives to judge us fairly. Men's standards of judgment are not sound, because they lack the perspective of eternity. Thus our dependence upon outward signs of success and our vulnerability to adverse judgments by others can divert us from establishing a relationship with the only One whose judgment ultimately matters very much.

The Apostle Paul wrote to the Romans, "We know that all things work together for good to them that love God." (Romans 8:28.) If we do all that is within our power to love God, then he has the power and the interest in us to see that all the circumstances of our lives will eventually "work together" for our best good.

This proposition is different from the Pollyanna-like assumption that because we are children of God, all things will work out for the best. More is required of us than that. For us, the requirement is to love God—to love him with all our heart, might, mind, and strength. That is no trivial task. For, "he that hath my commandments, and keepeth them, he it is that loveth me." (John 14:21.) It is a devotion that asks for all our hearts. Jesus asked Peter, "Wilt thou lay down thy life for my sake?" (John 13:38.) This may be what Joseph Smith meant in the sixth Lecture on Faith: "For a man to lay down his all, his character and reputation, his honor, and applause, his good name among men, his houses, his lands, his brothers and sisters, his wife and children, and even his own life also—counting all things but filth and dross for the excellency of the knowledge of Jesus Christ." This is the state of mind of one who offers "in sacrifice all that he has for the truth's sake, not even withholding his life, and believing before God that he has been called to make this sacrifice because he seeks to do his will." One who is prepared to establish this kind of relationship with God will "know, most assuredly, that God does and will accept his sacrifice and offering, and that he has not, nor will not seek his face in vain."[11]

Significantly, such single-minded devotion is within our control. It does not depend upon our talents, our heritage, our looks, or our intelligence. And the completeness of our love not only will not be judged by others—they are likely to know very little about it. For this is a love too private, too intimate and sacred to be seen of men, much less judged by them. There is only one judge, and on the fairness of his judgment we can surely rely. For "the keeper of the gate is the Holy One of Israel; and he employeth no servant there." (2 Nephi 9:41.)

If we love God in this sense, even though we are not perfect and even though we may not be thought of as "successful" or "excellent" by others, the promise is that all things will work together for our good. Through the miracle of the Atonement and through the grace and power of the Savior, this means that—if our repentance is complete—he will compensate for our failures, our sins, and our mistakes. It further means that he will perfect us—make us truly excellent—beyond our power to perfect ourselves.

All things working together for our good is very different from all things working together for our apparent success or excellence as measured by the standards of this world. Because his making us perfect enough to enjoy eternal life is the ultimate goal, we may need all things to work "for our good" in such a way that there are growing pains, tests, afflictions, and the purification by fire. For, he has said, "As many as I love, I rebuke and chasten." (Revelation 3:19.) This need for discipline may bring us experiences others would not judge to be big success stories. We may have encounters that are harsh, painful, and beyond our ability (let alone the ability of other people) to understand.

To develop a sufficiently independent relationship with God requires that the private world in which we dwell in communion with him transcend the other worlds we inhabit—the world of work, community life, friends, and even relationships in the Church. As we gain experience in that private and personal world, we will become less dependent upon the approval of others for our sense of personal worth. As that happens, we will come to understand what Hugh Nibley meant when he said: "I have always been furiously active in the Church, but I have . . . never held an office or rank in anything; I have undertaken many assignments given me by the leaders of the Church, and much of the work has been anonymous. No rank, no recognition, no anything. While I have been commended for some things, they were never the things which I considered most important— that was entirely a little understanding between me and my heavenly father, which I have thoroughly enjoyed, though no one else knows anything about it."[12]

An image suggesting this kind of private relationship with the Lord is described in a story by Robert Louis Stevenson. Stevenson tells of growing up in a part of England where darkness came early in the evening. He and his boyhood friends imitated British policemen by carrying small, tin "bull's eye" lanterns on their belts. Just for the fun of it, Stevenson and his friends made a game out of hiding the glowing lantern inside the front of their buttoned overcoats and then making their way along the dark paths as if they had no light with them. In Stevenson's words:

> When two of these [lads] met, there would be an anxious "Have you got your lantern?" and a gratified "Yes!" That was the shibboleth, and very needful, too; for, as it was the rule to keep our glory contained, none could recognize a lantern-bearer unless (like the polecat) by the smell. . . . The essence of this bliss was to walk by yourself in the black night, the slide shut, the top-coat buttoned, not a ray escaping, whether to conduct your footsteps or to make your glory public: a mere pillar of darkness in the dark; and all the while, deep down in the privacy of your fool's heart, to know you had a bull's-eye at your belt, and to exult and sing over the knowledge. . . .
> [One's] life from without may seem but a rude mound of mud; there will be some golden chamber at the heart of it, in which he dwells delighted; and for as dark as his pathway seems to the observer, he will have some kind of bull's-eye at his belt. [13]

Stevenson then describes the ultimate subjectivity of true joy, noting that other people simply cannot fully appreciate the innermost delights and sorrows in our lives. He suggests that if we could only experience forms of joy quickly perceived and acknowledged by others, that kind of joy would fall far short of the high forms of happiness and insight of which the human soul is capable.

As I think of Stevenson's description of our limited ability to communicate our deepest feelings through the limited power of verbal expression, I think of the little dog our family enjoyed during my own boyhood. When we would return from some extended time away, the little pup would be so glad to see us that he would run clear around the front lawn as fast as he could go; then he would come back and jump eagerly all over our legs, then take off again, racing around the lawn and back to us. He was just so happy that he couldn't express himself any better way.

Since our highest forms of joy (and, I suppose, our deepest moments of sorrow) are beyond the realm of ordinary speech, one great purpose served by music, art, poetry, and dance is to free us for a broader realm of personal expression. In Stevenson's words, "Only the poets find out where the joy resides, and give it a voice far beyond singing." Yet this private kind of joy, impossible to communicate objectively to others, is so significant in the human experience that, "To miss the joy is to miss all. In the joy of the actors lies the sense of any action. That is the explanation, that the excuse. To one who has not the secret of the lanterns, the scene [of the boys in the dark] is meaningless."[14]

If we understand the secret of the lanterns, we will not miss the joy that awaits us in discovering that all things do work together for good to those who love God. Others may not always understand what happens in this private world of our relationship with God. This means, of course, that they may be unlikely to applaud us or comfort us in those moments when we are most in need of being understood and appreciated. But if we love God, we have the assurance of knowing that he understands and sustains us, and the uninformed judgments of others, whether negative or positive, cannot come between us and God. As Paul said, "I am persuaded, that neither death, nor life, nor angels, nor principalities, nor powers, nor things present, nor things to come, nor height, nor depth, nor any other creature, shall be able to separate us from the love of God, which is in Christ Jesus our Lord." (Romans 8:38-39.)

If we were to let our thoughts be drawn out toward the heavens enough to transcend, even temporarily, the strains and limitations of daily life, we would be likely to hear the promptings of Him who overcame all things, assuring us that the promise is true: he will cause the circumstances of our lives to be for our ultimate blessing, if only we love him with all our hearts. There is no grading on a curve here. "He that overcometh, the same shall be clothed in white raiment; and I will not blot out his name out of the book of life, but I will confess his name before my Father and before his angels. . . . I know thy works; behold, I have set before thee an open door, and no man can shut it: for thou hast a little strength, and hast kept my word, and hast not denied my name. . . . Because thou hast kept the word of my patience, I also will keep thee from the hour of temptation, which shall come upon all the world. . . . Him that overcometh will I make a pillar in the temple of my God, and he shall go no more out: and I will write upon him the name of my God . . . and I will write upon him my new name." (Revelation 3:5, 8, 10, 12.)

To feel this assurance is to sense the reward of peace in this world and the promise of eternal life in the world to come. This is a more excellent way.

[1]*History of the People of Israel,* 1891, p. 415.

[2]Donald Kagan, et al., *The Western Heritage* (New York: Macmillan, 2nd ed., 1983), p. 46.

[3]Herbert Wallace Schneider, *The Puritan Mind* (Ann Arbor: The University of Michigan Press, 1958), pp. 34-35.

[4]Robert R. Palmer and Joel Colton, *A History of the Modern World* (New York: Alfred A. Knopf, 1963), p. 75.

[5]Thomas Greer, *A Brief History of the Western World* (New York: Harcourt Brace Janovich, 4th ed., 1983), p. 458.

[6]"The Choice," *Ensign,* November 1980, p. 21.

[7]Joseph F. Smith, *Gospel Doctrine* (Salt Lake City: Deseret Book, 1939), p. 285.

[8]*Christian Science Monitor,* October 13, 1977, p. 2.

[9]*Christian Science Monitor,* December 8, 1983, p. 46.

[10]"The Morality of Kinship," address delivered at Brigham Young University, November 15, 1983.

[11]*Lectures on Faith* 6:5, 7, 11.

[12]*Dialogue,* vol. 8, no. 1, p. 75.

[13]From Robert Louis Stevenson, "The Lantern-Bearers," quoted in William James, "On a Certain Blindness in Human Beings," *Talks to Teachers on Psychology and to Students on Some of Life's Ideals* (Cambridge, Mass.: Harvard University Press, 1983), pp. 135-36.

[14]James, *op. cit.*

Bruce C. Hafen has been president of Ricks College at Rexburg, Idaho, since 1978. A native of St. George, Utah, he received an associate degree from Dixie College, a bachelor's degree from Brigham Young University, and a J.D. from the University of Utah. He has taught at the J. Reuben Clark Law School at BYU and at the University of Utah College of Law. At BYU he was also associate director of the honors program and assistant to the president. He has published many professional papers as well as articles in Church publications and professional journals. In the Church he has been a Regional Representative of the Twelve and director of evaluation and planning for Church Correlation. He and his wife, the former Marie Kartchner, have seven children.

EXCELLENCE FOR ORDINARY PEOPLE

Elizabeth Haglund

Unlike virtue, which poets say is its own reward, excellence is everyone's reward. Everyone who creates excellence, and all who respond deeply to what others create—who feel, see, hear, touch, taste, wonder, and think—share in the joys of excellence. There is nothing abstract, unreal, or impractical about excellence. It is simply surpassing goodness in what we do, or what is done by others, that adds value to the experience of living. Every aspect of life may be burnished to excellence if we choose to have it that way. Even the most tedious and trivial tasks of everyday living are lifted to dignity and importance when we choose to make them excellent.

Who does not rejoice, at day's end, in the smooth, soothing comfort of a well-made bed? No wrinkles, no lumps, no pulled-out corners. Who does not celebrate a balanced checkbook, a stack of paid bills ready on time to go into the mail, a clean-swept garage, a mowed lawn, a kitchen set to rights after the evening meal, a loving letter written when it was needed? We don't have to be paragons to achieve this kind of excellence. What is called for is daily, quiet determination not to quit before we're finished—finished to whatever level of fineness the task deserves.

On our journey to useful, fulfilling selfhood, a taste for excellence is both the least and the most we can ask of ourselves. It is the least because there is no lasting satisfaction in any other way, and the most because no greater opportunity can come to us than living out our capabilities to the fullest.

When we are sufficiently touched by life and know something of its struggles—questions having no present answers, seemingly inscrutable injustices, the irrational along with the rational—we are led to discovery of a great simplicity: The business of living is not winning or losing. Life's joys are in giving our best to whatever we decide we must do. We give ourselves rewards by choosing, in duty and in love, to do well all that we are capable of doing. The process of trying, trying a little more, trying once again, and still again, reveals power in us that we could not have believed was there on the first try, or even on the next-to-last try. Like those we admire, we come to learn that circumstances notwithstanding, we can choose our own transcending best. Knowing that, we find it possible to bend to the realization that although we can't control the outcome of all that goes on around us, let alone the whole of life, we can by will and effort control the level of our own performance.

Our most spontaneous trying seems to begin and, sadly for many of us, to end in childhood. How tirelessly infants and children work to learn and accomplish. How they struggle to sit, stand, take a first uncoordinated step. Then suddenly they are running!

I watch my five-year-old great-niece get out her new jump rope and practice and practice without stopping, until with damp hair plastered to her flushed face, and nearly gasping for breath, she goes from beginning to end through a favorite jump-rope rhyme without a single misstep. No one taught her about excellence. She drove herself to it. Now that she knows how it feels, and likes the feeling, she likes herself, too. Probably she is not intellectually aware that excellence was her goal, but she knows she arrived at what she wanted to be able to do by trying again and again until she could do it perfectly. Simple. But not easy.

Richard L. Evans, originator of "The Spoken Word" for the Mormon Tabernacle Choir, and for more than forty-one years the voice of the profound truths he wrote and shared with radio and television audiences, agreed some years ago to present a tribute to J. Willard Marriott, for whom a building on the University of Utah campus was being named. It was my responsibility to provide the news media with advance information about the ceremonies and with a copy of Elder Evans' remarks. I made strenuous efforts to meet that obligation, but I was told that Elder Evans worked on his material right to the last minute and never released his work in advance. The several calls I made to his office produced polite but definite unresponsiveness. The morning of the scheduled presentation I made one more try. When I called Elder Evans' office, he happened to answer the phone. He listened to what I hoped was a persuasive plea, then said, "I can let you have my remarks in about two hours. But right now, I am still sandpapering." The finished work was indeed sandpapered—to a polish and shine so smooth that every thought came through in perfect clarity, and every carefully constructed phrase communicated beauty.

There is a price for such excellence—for every excellence, mundane or magnificent. The pain of sustained effort and the discipline of not giving up are the basics. The sweaty, trembly, inescapable suspicion that we have not yet reached the best that is in us, and that only more grinding effort will get us there is anguish. We want to stop, but stopping would cancel out all that we have done so far. So we persevere, spurred by the humbling understanding that unused gifts and overlooked capacities, however small, belittle ourselves and eventually hurt those who care most about us. Without wanting to, we sense that achieving quality is a reflection of how well we understand the gifts of life, how we feel about ourselves, what value we place on our own lives, and what obligation we feel to fulfill the potential that is in us. We may not, therefore, cave in.

We may have to be satisfied at first with modest aspirations—to make a beginning, master one task, increase one skill, multiply one talent. Then on the momentum of a small success, we find our courage and know we want to continue.

What if we set sail for excellence and fail? We will fail sometimes. We are not yet perfected, and we must be honest about accepting that reality without bitterness. Losses are the yardstick by which we measure what can be done better next time. Two thousand years ago the Roman philosopher Seneca told his followers, "Throughout the whole of life, one must continue to learn how to live." Is that not a way of urging that we expect and become prepared to overcome failure and inadequacies by extending our limits and reaching higher and higher as we learn?

My youngest sister, who was born blind, taught me many lessons about extending limits and making a handicap inconsequential. When she was about eleven years old, I took her to a Town Hall concert at which a Canadian pianist in her twenties, also blind from birth, was the performer. My sister, greatly gifted in music and already a well-trained pianist, insisted on arriving early for the concert to learn how the stage was arranged for the pianist's entrance. "For sure there will be a rubber mat leading from the Green Room to the piano," she said. When I checked, the rubber mat was there. "She will feel her way out to the piano by shuffling on that mat, just to prove she can find her own way. That's not fair to the audience," my sister said.

"When I give my Town Hall concert," she continued, "there will be no rubber mat. The stage curtain will be up as the audience comes in. Then just as it's time for the concert to begin, the curtain will be dropped, someone will quickly help me out to the piano, and when the curtain goes up again, there I'll be in my graceful chiffon dress, bowing to the audience. Then when I sit down at the piano and begin playing, the audience won't be thinking about my blindness. They can just think about my playing."

I marvel to this day at how her instincts and will, at age eleven, told her she need not be constantly jumping over the hurdle of her blindness. She would be a musician, not a blind musician, but one who would offer excellence to her audience.

Although all of us are capable of creating excellence in one form or another, the process of creation is not the only avenue to enjoyment of excellence. We have the words of the eighteenth-century French writer Voltaire to tell us, "By appreciation, we make excellence in others our own property."

What doors are opened by that idea! The rich worlds of literature, art, music, gardens, crafts, sports, people, architecture, travel, all worthy pursuits—all these and more may be ours for the choosing. And there's that word again: choosing. In one lifetime we cannot live out all our possibilities. To make room for excellence, we learn to select. We don't go to every movie, concert, or sports event. We don't acquire everything that momentarily catches our fancy. We don't fill our time responding to every invitation that comes along. To know excellence, we give up some things we want for things we want even more. There is an ongoingness in that process, and in time we get better and better at choosing how we will spend our time, energy, money, and attention. We acquire techniques for knowing excellence. We look, listen, touch, think, react, reflect, turn inward, experience. We sense new dimensions developing in us and fresh perspectives coming into play. We come to trust ourselves and know more of our own capacities. Excellence, we have already said, is everyone's reward, so we can free ourselves to go ahead and make it ours. We have learned the democracy of excellence and know that everyone may choose to participate in its pursuit.

On one otherwise unremarkable day I happened by a group of workmen assigned to hang an exhibit of portraits painted by Alvin Gittins. There were several dozen framed artworks to be arranged, and the workmen were unreservedly enjoying their task. They talked among themselves as they handled one after another of the striking portraits and openly responded to the powerful impact of the artist's work. They wondered aloud to each other, "Is this an internationally known painter? This is good stuff." A friend of Gittins who was supervising the exhibit came by in time to answer them. He said, "Alvin Gittins is greatly admired and well known among artists, but is probably not what you would call internationally known." "But he deserves to be," one of the men said. "So why isn't he?" The friend's answer was that

Gittins did not paint to become known. Public performance and public recognition were not the values he sought. Gittins' energy went into the quality of his work, not in seeking for attention. "He knows for himself when his work is good, and that is satisfaction enough" was the friend's summing up.

I think often of that incident. The workmen's enjoyment, their unabashed and unpretentious pleasure in what they were seeing, made clear that excellence speaks for itself and not just to a select few. Both creators and appreciators of excellence emerge from natural and unconstrained involvement with it.

On a snowy April evening I drove to Springville, Utah, to show my interest in a performing group that included two members of my family who live in Springville. This small Utah city, population possibly 12,000, is a community of farms, orchards, homes, a relatively new manufacturing plant, a well-established construction plant, and a main street whose merchants are slowly losing ground to the big shopping malls in the larger city only ten miles away. Not exactly the first place anyone might look for cultural excellence.

But Springville was given the gift, by one of its residents, of a small, fine art museum that not only presents exhibits of painting, sculpture, and crafts, but also a regular schedule of varied events in the performing arts. The art museum on this dismal evening was the setting for a choral concert presented by a group of Springville residents. Every Tuesday evening for an hour and a half, twenty neighbors get together for the sheer joy of singing together. Once a year they invite their friends to come hear what they have been doing.

The choir director is a graduate music student. His parents open their home for the choir rehearsals. Some of their music is performed to the accompaniment of a spinet harpsichord that the young music student and his father built. Members of the choir include a high school teacher, the principal of the high school, an attorney, several homemakers who also give piano, flute, or oboe lessons in their homes, a salesman, an executive in a construction firm, and a university faculty member.

I cannot be grateful enough to have been at the performance. I sat in the museum gallery reveling in the beauty the finely trained choir created as they sang Sibelius, Bach, Bruckner, Schumann, two original compositions by members of the choir—and songs by Cole Porter and Richard Rodgers as well. These people who each Tuesday forgo other important things to find pleasure, release, and renewal in their singing tell us, through their effort, that excellence has little to do with where we find it and everything to do with willingness to reach for it. It would have been an aching loss to have let a 100-mile drive and a late spring snowstorm keep me from this experience. The performers, who gave so much through their commitment to the joy of excellence, are all amateurs, in the sense of not being full-time professional singers. But they are not amateurs in excellence. Nor were the members of their audience amateurs. Despite the snow and the political mass meetings going on in the neighborhoods at the same time, more and more chairs had to be brought in to accommodate the large attendance. Excellent appreciators as well as excellent performers were plentiful.

A supreme and hard-won excellence, perhaps the most difficult excellence of all, is in the privilege of relationships with people. Relating to others and learning to relate well is the way we become fully dimensioned humans ourselves. The fact is, this excellence does not grow in solitude. However long the dedicated hours at the artist's easel, the cabinet-maker's workbench, the photographer's darkroom, or even in the kitchen putting together a glorious meal for family and friends, our connectedness to others requires special cultivation. Relationships grow best in what we do in concert with others. Never mind that the concert may sometimes be more discordant than harmonious. The work of relationships can still be in process, and as we learn to work at it, many new forms of excellence enter our lives. We need people and they need us.

Before we achieve the highest excellence in relating to

others, however, we need a loving relationship with ourselves. Jesus spoke of this in simplicity and plainness when he told us to love our neighbor *as* ourselves. Not in place of, not better than, but *as* ourselves. If we don't believe in and care about our own entities, we can't very well have anything to give to others, not in interest, in service, or in love.

We have as a base for proper love of self the recognition that we are each created as individuals, not as half of a pair or one-fifth of a family. We are separate, distinct, and worthwhile as ourselves. It is our responsibility to cultivate that self and make ourselves worthy of relating in excellence to others.

Instruction and inspiration for nurturing the best in ourselves are in Christ's sublime teachings throughout the New Testament. He counsels us in the strengths of meekness, mercy, peaceableness, slowness to anger, quickness to forgive, generosity in sharing, sacrifice, honesty, brotherly love—all the qualities of principled living. These traits, built into the everydayness of living, are the qualifications for excellence in relationships. We achieve them in patience, and we encourage their development by making time for our own growth—time to feel and know who we are, time to review our behaviors so we can know what we are doing with ourselves. Knowing ourselves, we can trust our responses to others.

In the processes of thinking *as* and *for* ourselves, we prepare for increasingly productive service in society. Part of being adult is doing our own thinking. True, we live in a society and cannot be immune to what goes on around us, but we think our own thoughts. Society does not think; only individuals do that. Thinking for and about ourselves helps us to know if we really want ourselves as we are, or if we wish we could exchange that self for some other. Dr. Edward Teller, the great physicist, has often referred to the "unused excellencies which lie dormant in almost everyone." In introspection we may discover our excellencies and come to want those we may lift from dormancy. Then we can reach out in wholeness to give love to others.

In her book *Families*, Jane Howard writes: "Call it a clan, call it a network, call it a tribe, call it a family. What- ever you call it, whoever you are, you need one. You need one because you are human. You didn't come from nowhere. Before you, around you, and presumably after you, too, there are others. Some of these others . . . must matter a lot to you, and if you are very lucky to one another. Their welfare must be nearly as important to you as your own. Even if you live alone, even if your solitude is elected and ebullient, you still cannot do without a clan or a tribe." (New York: Simon and Schuster, 1978, pp. 260-61.)

Within our clans, tribes, or families we step out of the small world of "I" and "me" into engrossingly larger worlds. But excellence in relationships no longer allows us to live exclusively with people "just like us," with people who come from backgrounds like ours, share the same values, are at the same stage of life, belong to the same clubs and groups. In re- lationships, the magic is in the mix. Learning about the good in others, the excitement of diversity, the values in other cultures, the color and beauty in lives different from our own thrusts us into entirely new ways of being excellent.

The fact that my family moved from Utah to New York when I was a child made this realization easy for me. I was raised in a Brooklyn neighborhood that allowed for friend- ships with the families of Irish Catholic "cops," Jewish den- tists, Presbyterian auto dealers, and Italian storekeepers. Many of the things that mattered to my friends' families were curiously different from what mattered to my family. The foods they ate were different, as were their holidays, their forms of worship, their politics. (And Brooklyn children, even very young ones, were partisan about politics.) Hap- pily, that diversity was accompanied by neighborliness, not exclusiveness, and we came to share easily in each other's lives. We shared fortune and misfortune. We exchanged meals, stayed in a neighbor's home when a new baby was born in ours, borrowed tools, and profited from the skills of other families' fathers, mothers, and older brothers. I am deeply indebted to the opportunities of my Brooklyn child- hood.

I do not make snap judgments so quickly in circumstances that are new to me. I am not frightened of ways
that at first seem strange. I can be open longer to the ideas of
others. I am more inclined to examine what I believe before I
reject the values important to others. I need not like differing codes, much less adopt them, but acknowledging that
they exist and may have some right to exist reinforces my
own convictions. Application of traits like these sweetens
family life, working associations, neighborhoods, and even
whole communities.

A group of sociologists once studied skid-row society in
Denver and Chicago. Their surprising discovery was that
there is something true about that culture that we only say is
true about our middle-class world. People care about one
another on skid row. They go the distance with one another.
They help in difficult circumstances. They regard themselves as their brothers' keeper. One of the sociologists
said, "You know, if I didn't have a family, I think I'd live
there." There is goodness and sadness in what was found in
that study. It's good that people who have so little else can
be excellent in relationships. But how sad that there is truth
in the perception that the rest of us don't quite measure up to
the brotherhood opportunities.

I wonder why we save love and support for such small
circles of influence. The wondrous thing about love is that it
renews itself as fast as we can spend it.

A primary joy of life is acceptance, approval, the sense
of companionship and appreciation from others. The need
for fellowship with other humans is as deep as the need for
food. In our very natures, there is not only the desire to receive love from others, but also an inner necessity to give
love. The poet Robert Browning wrote: "There is an answer
to the passionate longings of the heart for fulness, and it is
this: you must in all things live outside yourself in love. That
is God's life and it ought to be our lives. In Him it is accomplished and perfect; but in all created things it is to be
learned slowly and against great difficulty."

The reach for excellence culminates in generous cultivation of the capacity to love, to relate to others, to under-

stand, to share. This is the excellence to which all others
lead. To know this excellence is to know the ultimate joy of
excellence.

*Elizabeth Haglund, special assistant to the president of the University of Utah,
was reared and educated in suburban New York City. She attended Hunter
College and Columbia University, and worked as an advertising copywriter for
John Wiley and Sons. For many years she was affiliated with National Broad-
casting Corporation in publicity and personnel capacities. Now a resident of
Salt Lake City, she was executive director of public relations at the University
of Utah before transferring to her present position. She has served on the general
boards of the Sunday School and the Young Women's Mutual Improvement
Association, and has been active in community affairs, including United Way,
the Utah Chamber of Commerce, and the Utah Endowment for the Hu-
manities.*

EXCELLENCE—AN ISSUE OF VALUES

Stanford Cazier

In the summer of 1980, my wife and I had one of the choicest experiences of our married life when we spent a month in Europe. The stimulus for this experience was the graciousness of a couple, both friends and former students. He was the landscape architect of the Aga Khan, and they had a townhouse in Versailles that they generously made available to us.

We saw everything in and around Paris that most tourists see and a few things they do not. One highlight was planned—a trip to Chartres Cathedral. It was more than we had expected. As a graduate student, I studied medieval civilization and philosophy and had read Henry Adams' classic, *Mont Saint Michael and Chartres*, in preparation for the trip. What we witnessed was beyond our expectation. The symbolism of allegory expressed in architecture, sculpture, and stained glass was masterful.

During the next nine days, we drove through southern France, Switzerland, and southwest Germany from Munich to Frankfurt. Each day had its special wonders. Finally, after driving down the Rhine on the last afternoon of our trip by car, we headed back to Paris. It rained off and on most of the way, and the drive was uneventful, especially after nightfall, until we encountered an experience we had not anticipated.

Around ten o'clock in the evening, a road sign indicated that Reims was just a few kilometers ahead. In our weariness, we had momentarily forgotten that we would be passing through Reims, the home of one of the great medieval cathedrals of Europe. While we were very tired and had been almost satiated with stimuli from the day's experience, we could not pass through Reims without stopping. We cannot describe our feelings as we approached the magnificent cathedral lighted as if in a haloed mist. As I recall, we were there until almost midnight feasting on that inspiring sight. At Reims as at Chartres, we knew we had been in the presence of excellence. At this point, one might ask, Why are some things considered excellent and others not?

The word *excellence* evokes images of what we recognize as superior. Occasionally, excellence has been applied to that which is greater or larger in quantity. More appropriately, excellence speaks to the substance of that which is valued intrinsically.

Like a closely associated term, *quality*, excellence does not lend itself to easy definition. And, like quality, while we may not be able to define excellence, we are generally able to recognize it when we are confronted with it, just as when we discovered Chartres and Reims—one in the full light of day and the other in a rainy mist at midnight.

Early in my study of the Bible, I learned of the Lord's concern for excellence when "Abel offered unto God a more excellent sacrifice." (Hebrews 11:4.) Cain withheld from the Lord that which was of greater worth and thereby charted a course that led him down a dark path.

From this biblical account, excellence, it would seem, has a strong linkage to that which is moral and can never be associated with any dimension of the immoral. Strictly from a military perspective, Adolf Hitler, directly or indirectly, accomplished some rather dazzling strategic and tactical maneuvers in the late 1930s and early 1940s. Although these maneuvers were accorded recognition as being brilliant, they cannot be equated with excellence.

Most examples of excellence display a high order of intellectual energy. So while there are few instances of excellence without concomitant mental rigor, there can be cognitive brilliance with only a limited trace of excellence.

The German poet Goethe said that "life divided by reason leaves a remainder." Excellence requires the presence of the denominator, but it is not fulfilled without the remainder. There is more than intellect in excellence.

The syllogistic pyrotechnics of Abelard's twelfth century may be compared with a grand masters' chess tournament or even with high-level number crunching by the best computer hackers of our own day. Excellence can be appropriately applied to a select array of activities, however amoral some of them may be. But unless the human spirit is somehow lifted by the experience, a significant dimension of excellence is missing from the equation.

The excellence that elevates is closer to the relationship Robert Pirsig insisted exists between quality and caring: "Care and Quality are internal and external aspects of the same thing. A person who sees Quality and feels it as he works is a person who cares. A person who cares about what he sees and does is a person who's bound to have some characteristics of Quality." (*Zen and the Art of Motorcycle Maintenance*, New York: William Morrow & Company, 1974, p. 275.)

Excellence, however, has to be more embracing than mere pride and commitment in the quality of one's craftmanship. Excellence at this level represents too much focus on the "I" and not enough on Martin Buber's "thou" or the broad spectrum of "others" in our lives that Christ called us to serve. The human spirit cannot be made to soar in isolation. When our efforts assist in lifting the spirits of others, we too have a possibility of soaring; then we approach excellence in its purest form.

The compelling popularity of *In Search of Excellence: Lessons from America's Best-Run Companies* by Thomas J. Peters and Robert H. Waterman is not a function of new refinement of analytical techniques applied to business management, but rather the pervasive bone-deep concern for the dignity of every individual. In this book the focus is on people, and attention to them and concern for their welfare appears to be the bottom line in the best-run companies. "Treating people—not money, machines, or minds—as the natural resource may be the key to it all," they conclude.

In the crucial years of my collegiate youth, I encountered a man who embodied the kind of excellence that kept *people* in the forefront. Lowell L. Bennion was the director of the LDS Institute of Religion at the University of Utah, and by the time I had met him, he had already established a place for himself in the forefront of Church education. I was impressed that he had obtained his doctorate at Strasbourg, and that he was an equal to critics and scholars in many disciplines and was often included in dialogues and debates with eminent scholars.

My associations with him, however, soon taught me that none of these academic achievements were primary in his value system. Human relationships counted for much more than academic status. The kindness with which he treated secretaries, students, custodians, and neighbors was the first lesson I learned. Then I discovered it was more than kindness. He took them seriously. He listened to them. He invited students to criticize, even revise, his manuscripts. He turned to homespun neighbors as his source for wisdom. He respected books and scholars, yes, but he also gleaned knowledge from daily life and ordinary people.

Later I discovered a third level of his excellence: compassion and concern. His life seemed to center around the disadvantaged, the immigrant, the widowed, the financially distressed, the emotionally distraught. Despite the impelling magnet that ideas and analysis held for him, and despite the love he had for teaching and writing, people meant more. He kept an active list of people's needs in his mind. He welcomed their requests. He inquired about their burdens. He devoted his own time and resources to help them. He multiplied his efforts by guiding students to similar concerns and service. Finally, in a second career, he turned his whole life to community service.

His books are still being written. He sandwiches them in between people concerns. And those of us who read them find an excellence that is more than cerebral. Also—and this is a most important legacy—he has passed these qualities on to his children.

The personal paradigm of excellence can be compared to its more impersonal expression in the institutions of business, industry, and education. America, not so many years ago, prided itself on its superiority (particularly quantitative) in most quarters of human endeavor. What country could match the American genius for business and industry? Our assembly lines were the envy of the world. Our captains of industry had helped to create a standard of living that was transcendent. Literacy was almost universal, and opportunities for a college education were unparalleled.

However, in the past twenty-five years we have begun to hear footsteps over our shoulders. Several countries, including Germany, France, and Japan, have successfully challenged our business preeminence. Japan, in particular, with few natural resources other than the most important one—human—has produced hundreds of products that are better and cheaper than their counterparts in the United States. Simultaneously, there has been a steady decline in the Scholastic Aptitude Test (SAT) scores for high school graduates. Using just these two important indices—industrial productivity and SAT scores—America seems to be slipping from its pinnacle of excellence.

As a result, there has been almost frenetic activity on the business and educational fronts in an effort to recoup our lost laurels. Seminars on productivity and better management techniques are frequently sponsored by businesses and universities. Americans have even a greater concern for the apparent erosion of our educational luster. A Gallup poll conducted in 1983 ranked concern for the quality of education well ahead of industrial productivity.

Early last year those concerns were crystallized in the report of the National Commission on Excellence in Education entitled *A Nation at Risk: The Imperative for Educational Reform,* which gave its now well-known warning that "the educational foundations of our society are presently being eroded by a rising tide of mediocrity." Not since Sputnik has America focused such attention on education as it did in 1983. As was the case in 1957, a clarion call went out for new rigor in the basics: reading, writing, and computation. While *A Nation at Risk* struck a responsive chord in the national consciousness, many of us agreed with former U.S.

Commissioner of Education Harold Howe II when he wrote, "There are a lot of problems, but there are also a lot of good schools out there and a lot of kids learning. I think American education has a cold; most people think it has the flu. It certainly doesn't have the pneumonia that the commission has suggested."

The same incentives that led to the creation of the National Commission on Excellence in Education also led to the publication of an unprecedented number of reports by other agencies. In May, *Making the Grade* was published by the Twentieth Century Fund as a report on the Fund's Task Force on Federal Elementary and Secondary Education Policy. The month of May also witnessed the publication of *Academic Preparation for College: What Students Need to Know and Be Able to Do*, a report of the College Board's Educational Equality Project.

In June, the Education Commission of the States Task Force on Education for Economic Growth produced *Action for Excellence*. In the fall, an additional document only added fuel to the fire. It was the report of the National Science Board Commission on Precollege Education in Mathematics, Science and Technology, entitled *Educating Americans for the 21st Century*.

In September, the two most compelling publications of the year appeared. Far and away the most comprehensive study of public education came from the pen of John Goodlad, former dean of the Graduate School of Education at UCLA. His book, entitled *A Place Called School: Prospects for the Future*, reflected nearly a decade of close scrutiny of public schools across America and represented the most ambitious project of its type ever undertaken.

The other September publication was a book entitled *High School: A Report on Secondary Education in America*, written by Ernest Boyer, president of the Carnegie Foundation for the Advancement of Teaching. While not uncritical, it provided a decidely hopeful view of education. Boyer uncovered some examples of excellent learning experiences and found impressive improvements already underway.

Moreover, his is probably the only study that attempts to explain how education can contribute to a more interesting and thoughtful life—and not just a more competitive one.

While the reports differed in many respects, they did tend to appeal for a core curriculum with emphasis on the basics and special emphasis on English and mathematics. No one can deny the need for the highest level of literacy that one can achieve for all of our students. And if they are to cope with and be productive in a high technology society, they will need computational skills. They will also need to feel comfortable with the bases of knowledge acquisition. However important an appreciation of these basics is, they are, after all, the *tools* of learning.

Conspicuously absent from the 1983 reports were references to the ends of education. Most of these reports defined educational excellence in terms of keeping up and improving the competitive edge in world markets—the stakes being economic, with our living standards in the balance. Most do not avow that learning may be pursued for its own sake. As Lawrence Cremin of Columbia University reflected, "The several reports issued in 1983 had very little to say about the development of *character* and about what *values* should be taught and by what means." Competition requires a value system to guide its energy.

It is one thing to have the expertise to build a bridge or a nuclear reactor or to engage in genetic engineering. It is quite another to be able to decide whether the bridge or reactor *should* be built and under what conditions genetic engineering should take place. The former represents the means of education; the latter, the ends. And the latter are derivative judgments made by a host of people who reflect the best in our cultural heritage and human relationships.

If the spate of commission and committee reports focusing on the improvement of education seemed indifferent to the development of character and shared values, this deficiency was just as pervasive in documents and events attendant to the celebration of America's bicentennial. However, the year 1976 was also Johns Hopkins University's centennial, and participants in the celebration of that university's one hundred years of existence included some very distinguished individuals who addressed the importance of values.

Malcolm G. Scully summarized the Johns Hopkins University celebration for the *Chronicle of Higher Education* in its March 1, 1976, issue under the title "After the First 100 Years, Wither the U.S. University?" Scully underscored the consensus of the group that "the war in Viet Nam, the Watergate scandal, and the recent revelations of bribery by some major corporations have produced a 'crisis of values' that the universities must address." David Rodgers, president of the Robert Wood Johnson Foundation, asked the question, "In a world where family structure, religious values, or other guidelines formerly used by society as benchmarks seem to be faltering, where is the university taking the lead in developing sensible new touchstones which can make us wish to be human, educated and adult?" Father Theodore M. Hesburgh, president of Notre Dame, observed that "society expects less of us than the salvation of the world, the answer to every possible problem, the panacea of a new world. [However,] we have learned, both society and the university, that values are important: personal values, family values, business and professional values, national and international values." Representative John Brademas from Indiana capitalized on what Father Hesburgh said: "What are our values and how do we teach them in today's America?" He went on to say, "The issue of values in the university is a mine field, but universities cannot ignore it." How significant are values? In a year of searching for renewed excellence, these leaders celebrating the excellence of Johns Hopkins University would yearn for values.

As Americans moved past the celebration of our bicentennial and into the first year of the third century of our existence, a veritable floodgate opened, revealing a broad concern that we were sailing on relatively uncharted seas and that our public life, especially our universities, appeared to have a very loose tiller.

Early in 1977, Howard R. Bowen, former chancellor of the Claremont College Group and currently a professor of education and economics in the Claremont Graduate School, published a widely heralded book entitled *Investment in Learning: the Individual and Social Value of American Higher Education.* On the whole, Dr. Bowen makes a very persuasive case that investment in learning, in human capital, pays high personal and professional dividends, and that substantial benefits accrue to society as a whole. However, there is an ambivalent, if not alarming, note also sounded in this important book. "College seemingly does not have a marked impact on attitudes of altruism and philanthrophy leading to kindness, sympathy, unselfishness, sociability, or friendliness toward other individuals," he said. In addition, "Another obvious warning against too easy acceptance of college influence as favorable to the development of sound values is that academic cheating, shoplifting, and vandalism have been on the increase on most campuses in the past decade."

In September 1977, *Psychology Today* published a review of Alexander Astin's *Four Critical Years: Effects of College on Beliefs, Attitudes, and Knowledge.* Astin's book was a longitudinal study that had monitored 200,000 students in 300 institutions during their undergraduate experience. Among the findings of Astin's significant study, as pointed out in the review, was that college students "showed declining interest in philosophies of life and idealistic values and a growing interest in such materialistic goals as wealth and status. . . . In general, the freshmen responses showed declining idealism and increasing cynicism and materialism, particularly during the last five years."

I like to think that this specific need—the need for idealism—is where Latter-day Saints have a contribution to make. Many LDS students still have the wholesomeness, the dedicated vision of service, the definition of purpose that can guide them past the crevices of materialism and indulgence. I do not fool myself into believing that they are the only ones so endowed or that self-interest has not diverted some

Latter-day Saints into corruption, but my daily contact with students in this remote corner of the world makes me hopeful—hopeful particularly because these students have a paramount commitment to values.

In the October 3, 1977, issue of the *Chronicle of Higher Education,* Susan Resneck Parr, an associate professor of English at Ithaca College, particularized her concern that "teachers who challenge their students to think about values are fighting an entire culture." After indicating that the Johnnies and Janes of this world cannot "spell, write clear prose, or think logically and critically," Professor Parr stated that while this illiteracy was "terrifying," she was convinced that "there is even a more serious problem facing academe and society as a whole: students are also indifferent to the question of *values.* . . . I am dismayed by the pervasive lack of concern about moral issues." Part of Professor Parr's "terror" was associated with the fact that the students' "indifference is a consciously chosen, almost often self-righteous stance." Many of her students told her that "since the world is corrupt, there is no point in bothering about anything other than their own personal and immediate well-being."

It is an interesting but less than significant coincidence that two of America's most influential writers have the same name—John Gardner. Two of their most recent efforts extend that coincidence but with sobering significance in addressing a common issue—America's "values crisis."

John W. Gardner, founder of Common Cause and former Secretary of Health, Education, and Welfare, stood back from the world of politics and social action to assess the attitudes, beliefs, and values that are the underpinning of that action and finds us wanting. In his book *Morale,* he argues persuasively that as a nation, we are seriously adrift because we are bereft of shared beliefs and values—shorn of fundamental purpose.

John Gardner, the brilliant and prolific novelist, turned essayist to indict current art and criticism for their lack of moral focus. In his provocative *On Moral Fiction,* this gifted novelist insists that "true art is moral," but then boldly denounces most art, especially fiction, as being "either trivial or false."

The significance of the Gardners' shared sense of concern stems, in part, from the forceful articulations of a serious pathological phenomenon. The loss of shared beliefs and values and the absence of purpose can render us susceptible to cynicism and disillusionment, which in turn can "destroy our will"—the basis for meaningful existence.

Robert Coles, the eminent psychiatrist at Harvard University, whose prolific writings include the monumental *Children of Crisis*, has not been hesitant to address the issue of moral development, and the theme emerges in many of his books and articles, often in explicit form. In the September-October 1977 issue of *Today's Education*, he wrote to the question, "What About Moral Sensibility?" In his statement, he speaks to the insidious effects of not facing up to the question of moral sensibility—of how the modes and mores of society can blunt the concerns of an "ethically sensitive boy whose moral sensibility moved him to think of others." Often, in the classroom and in the larger society, we are the conscious and unconscious accomplices of various "kinds of repression—of ways children learn to repress a sense of fairness, social justice, concern for people different from themselves." Dr. Coles concludes that "even the teaching of arithmetic and English, those basics, can be made vivid and concrete and terribly significant to children if they are connected to the everyday moral and ethical dilemmas all of us struggle with as citizens."

Finally, the Carnegie Foundation for the Advancement of Teaching published a most stimulating document in 1977, entitled *Missions of the College Curriculum*, with primary focus being given to the improvement of general education. In particular, the report called for three areas that should receive special attention and effort: (1) the improvement of basic skills; (2) more significant connections between the world of formal education and the world of work; and (3) a new stress on moral values. The commentary read: "The campus can and should be an ethically stimulating environment. The ethical ideals of the academic community are high and can even be a model for the society at large. They need, however, to be made more explicit . . . more conscientiously observed."

The question could be readily asked, Was 1977, the first year of our third century as an independent country, aberrant, with inordinate attention to the question of values? The answer would have to be a categorical no! Many who have spoken or written since that year have also reiterated concern over the apparent thinness of our moral resolve and of the lack of clarity and consensus over purpose in our public and private lives. But there are also voices and pens that suggest that there are models of resolve, affirmation of purpose, and articulation of values if we have the desire to seriously entertain them.

In their book *In Search of Exellence,* Peters and Waterman conclude that "every excellent company we studied is clear on what it stands for, and takes the process of value shaping seriously. In fact, we wonder whether it is possible to be an excellent company without clarity on values and without having the right sorts of values." "Now, why is all of this important?" they ask. "Because so much of excellence in performance has to do with people's being motivated by compelling, simple—even beautiful—values."

It is compellingly reinforcing to discover that the pervasive concern for people and values in Peters and Waterman's *Search for Excellence* also underscores probably the most important trend enumerated in John Naisbitt's bestseller *Megatrends,* the desire for "high touch" to complement, if not counterpoint, our "high tech" society:

"Technology and our human potential are the two great challenges and adventures facing humankind today. The great lesson we must learn from the principle of high tech/ high touch is a modern version of the ancient Greek ideal—*balance.* We must learn to balance the material wonders of technology with the spiritual demands of our human nature.

"Readers of the *Trend Report*'s education section noticed a curious phenomenon for volume two of the 1980 report. During the exact same time period that articles on education appeared throughout the nation reporting widespread use of the computer in the schools, a wave of stories appeared about either reviving religion in the schools or about teaching values. . . . Conclusion? Again it is high tech/high touch. As computers begin to take over some of the basics of education, schools will more and more be called upon to take responsibility for teaching values and motivation, if not religion." (New York: Warner Books, 1982, p. 47.)

If basic values are to reform our behavior, we need to be attentive to balance in our lives, not let the dazzle and comfort of modern living blind us to "the spiritual demands of our human nature." Paul the Apostle gloried both in the rational and the moral: "Prove all things; hold fast that which is good." (1 Thessalonians 5:21.)

We need to cultivate a sense of discrimination in all that we think, say, and do if we hope to evince excellence in our lives. We need the reminder of Paul's counsel: "All things are lawful for me, but all things are not expedient: . . . all things edify not." (1 Corinthians 10:23.) "I would have you wise unto that which is good, and simple concerning evil." (Romans 16:19.)

The capacity to exercise discrimination implies the power to make choices, to exercise free will. Without free agency, there would be no possibility of fulfilling the spiritual demands of our human nature. Few would quarrel with such an elemental principle. What is not so elemental is the unfortunate confusion between free agency and freedom. The former is essential to the latter, but only the proper exercise of agency can guarantee freedom. That which does not edify may wear away the underpinning of our freedom. Active pursuit of truth, beauty, and goodness brings a sense of harmony and peace.

I recently heard of a bright man from a Communist country who had the rare opportunity to visit relatives in a free Western country. As part of those few precious days, he traveled to a nearby world cultural center where he roamed the streets with abandon. Months later, at home and re-united with his family in his dictatorial confinement, he was confidentially asked by visiting westerners if he did not ache to escape with his family to freedom. He hesitated. Then he admitted that for himself and his wife, he wished it. But for his children, he feared it. Stunned, the westerners asked why. He replied that his walks through those streets deeply disappointed him as he encountered open pornography, the drug scene, and crass materialism. He had hoped that Communist propaganda about the democratic countries was a distortion, but he was offended by the blatant evidences of corruption in the West.

Christ said: "I am come that they might have life, and that they might have it more abundantly" (John 10:10), for the rich, full, and excellent life of which we are capable. And we are capable. After all, "What is man, that thou art mindful of him? . . . Thou hast made him a little lower than the angels, and hast crowned him with glory and honour." (Psalm 8:4-5.)

Our capability, freedom, and worth grow with the consistency and quality of our choices. Too many of us become discouraged, frustrated, and, more serious, jaded by results of our choices. Some, unfortunately, proceed "past feeling" in the casualness, even carelessness, of the exercise of agency. The abundant, excellent, free life is then beyond them. They are then bound by a condemnation that is unique. Dostoyevsky captures that condemnation with special eloquence in his novel *Crime and Punishment:* "No penalty can be so severe as that imposed by the human soul upon itself."

We are not fated to engage in self-condemnation, but to experience moments of exquisite joy, if we will it. That joy, if life is to have zest and meaning, is not a prize or product to be picked up at the end of the journey, but is more of a by-product. It is the tone of the process of living.

Joy is not necessarily to be found in the complex nor the profound things of life, but rather in the simple, easy yoke. A touch of excellence can be found during tender moments with a companion, in the times we extend our substance to those in need, in quietly listening to a troubled soul, in delicately nurturing children and older people, in realizing a wisp of wisdom through feeling experiences. Unless we serve in the vineyard, neither we nor that which requires cultivation can grow and experience joy. This is germane to excellence, for excellence is more than intellect.

In life many, many things will properly command our interest, and as we grow and tune our eyes, ears, hearts, and souls, we come to know that which is to be respected, that which deserves admiration; and if we truly reach beyond ourselves, we can come to know reverence and even worship.

Some will say that the values I have espoused belong only in church. Some values do, but many can be taught even in public institutions without compromising their integrity. More than thirty years ago, C. S. Lewis chided educational institutions for not taking more seriously the obligation to help students in their moral development:

"They see the world around them swayed by emotional propaganda—they have learned from tradition that youth is sentimental—and they conclude that the best thing they can do is to fortify the minds of young people against emotion. My own experience as a teacher tells an opposite tale. For every one pupil who needs to be guarded from a weak excess of sensibility, there are those who need to be awakened from a slumber of cold vulgarity. The task of the modern educator is not to cut down jungles, but to irrigate deserts. The right defense against false sentiments is to inculcate just sentiments. By starving the sensitivity of our pupils, we only make them easier prey to the propagandist when he comes, for famished nature will be avenged, and a hard heart is no infallible protection against the soft head."

We are a value-laden society. We do ourselves an injustice if we do not acknowledge that we value justice, mercy, freedom, loyalty, honesty, courage, patience, gratitude, courtesy. The list could be extensive. Few would deny the assertion of John W. Gardner that "values are not only fiercely defended but lied about, distorted, and flagrantly betrayed. They decay and revive. People fight and die over them; lives are ruined or ennobled; blood is spilled. Many people betray in action the values they profess." To ignore this reality in academe is to diminish a responsibility not only to expand minds but also to enlarge the human spirit.

Numerous articles have been written over the past few years championing the idea that value or moral education can be approached within the halls of academe without abrogating cultural diversity, scientific objectivity, and other canons sacred to public higher education and at the same time avoiding indoctrination often associated with moral or value education. The thrust of these articles has not been to teach the student what things he or she should value, but to establish the means by which the individual student comes to have moral sensibility and to make moral judgments; in short, to engage creatively and cognitively in the most mature way possible in the valuation process.

Some educators feel that the issue of values should be left exclusively to the family and the church. David E. Purpel and Kevin Ryan, in their book *Moral Education . . . It Comes with the Territory,* do not agree. They submit that in "one way or another moral education does, in fact, go on continuously in our public schools, either as part of the 'overt curriculum' or part of the 'hidden curriculum.'" They give as examples the fact that students sometimes debate the "validity of abortion in a biology class, or they discuss the appropriateness of revolution when studying American colonial history," and they are often asked to deal with the moral dilemma that Huckleberry Finn faced in his relation with Jim, "the runaway slave." They go on to say that "at least as significant as the formal curriculum is the quantity of moral education implicit in the activities of formal and informal school organization—each has the potential for communicating significant moral messages, issues and dimensions." The final appeal of these two authors is that "educators and the general public must realize that in our schools moral education is an unavoidable responsibility. It comes with the territory."

Finally, whether in the cathedral or the classroom, excellence as an issue of values unfolds through a developed capacity for discrimination, for respect, admiration, reverence, and even worship. Joy, born of the fruits of the Spirit through fundamental service, is also a manifestation of excellence, not unlike a work of art simplified in a harmony of balance and design. Excellence is a pursuit and not an arrival or merely an acquisition. Excellence is dynamic, not a formula to be applied in all circumstances. As our understanding increases with experience, so will our appreciation of excellence.

Stanford Cazier has been president of Utah State University in Logan since 1979. From 1971-79 he was president of California State University at Chico, and prior to that he was on the history faculty and vice-provost at Utah State University. Dr. Cazier received his bachelor's and master's degrees from the University of Utah and a Ph.D. in history from the University of Wisconsin. He has served in teaching and executive capacities in the Church, including gospel doctrine teacher in four wards. He and his wife, the former Shirley Anderson, have three sons.

SEEKING THE JOY OF EXCELLENCE

Crawford Gates

The creations of God provide ultimate prototypes for excellence. The spectrum of incredible creativity from the hand and mind of the Creator gives rich evidence of the great care and precision with which his works are prepared.

This is true from the magnificence of the swirling galaxies to the calculated laws that govern the motion of electrons, and the infinite variety in between, all marked by the multifaceted characteristics of order, purpose, and beauty. When we perceive even a minute part of this teeming virtuosity of creative excellence, we are moved to stand in awe, and to worship and to say in our hearts "Blessed is he!" When the Lord surveyed his own efforts, he commented in what seems to be an extremely modest understatement, "It is good." My small and naive view would be, still understated, "It's incredibly marvelous!"

If I were seeking an example of excellence in creativity, I would survey some part of the millions of miracles that make up this gorgeous planet on which we dwell. Or I would gaze with wonder on the blade of grass, or the imponderables of gravity, light, and electricity, or the fertilization of an ovum. There is so much we cannot grasp, and what we do perceive seems so small and incomplete. Yet it is complete enough to suggest the appropriateness of profound respect, adoration, and desire for oneness with the source of such beauty and wonder. The glories of God are many indeed, and among these glories are his patterns of excellence in everything he touches. And because we are his and like him in some small measure, we too thirst after excellence in our limited pursuits. The attainment of excellence, even in modest dimensions, provides its own rich rewards with an additional bonus frequently appearing as a happy side effect: Joy!

If God is our prime example of excellence, he is not the only one. There are some brilliant human examples from whom we can take encouragement and motivation, even if we cannot expect to reach their substantial achievements.

Take, for instance, Johann Sebastian Bach, one of the highest of geniuses. Of course, he did not perceive himself as such. Even his own brilliant sons, four of whom also made lasting musical achievements, did not recognize the towering stature of their German burgher father. He was thought of as a substantial but sometimes old-fashioned church organist who exhibited some highly unusual improvisational capacities at the organ and harpsichord. He lived out his somewhat obscure life in a middle-sized German city and was involved in the musical life of one of the Lutheran churches of his community, teaching, composing, and performing the duties appropriate to his time and place.

A look at just one area of Bach's prodigious output, the cantata, provides some understanding of his amazing creativity. The cantatas, almost three hundred in number, were written mostly for performance at St. Thomas' church during the three-hour Sunday services. His resources were organ, harpsichord, and a handful of singers and instrumentalists, some of whom were objects of his complaints for their musical limitations. The members of the congregation must have had some perception as to what he was saying musically as well as textually, or he would not have had the heart to crank out this series of incredible masterpieces, week after week, during the twenty-seven years of his residency as Cantor of St. Thomas. He did not look upon them as masterpieces, but he did wish to serve his congregation to the best of his ability, and he did wish to give honor to the glory of God with his own "modest" skill, as he said occasionally on the cantata manuscripts.

Bach considered himself a skilled craftsman, not unlike the men who built his organ, violin, and harpsichord. He did not know that he was to become JOHANN SEBASTIAN BACH, that giant, that consummate musical genius who turned the art of fugue into the Art of Fugue, and who turned the evolving church cantata into a series of singularly transcendent spiritual expressions that confirm anew that he was inspired of God. BACH! Even the name sounds like a multi-faceted diamond. And certainly he was such. The excellence of his output was marked by textures that never seemed wrong, but always were unfolding with the right note at the right time. His music had a sense of inevitability. The next chord had to be C-sharp minor, the next entrance could be nothing but up an interval of a fourth from the previous one, the next turn of a repetitive figure just the right one to give freshness to the unified continuum—each line ever new, ever a delight, but continually related to what had gone before and what was coming after, the trip an exhilaration for the ear, mind, and spirit. And his musical messages have continued to enrich the perceptive mind and heart through decades and centuries, across national and cultural boundaries. Bach glorified God in his music, both by his intent and by the transcendent power of its reality. The music is excellent in its lofty spiritual conception and in the technical mastery that expresses it.

We may marvel at Bach's creativity, but we lack understanding of his creative process because he and his family and associates left little firsthand evidence of it. Not so with Mozart. The record abounds with testimonies that music came into this mind ready-made, almost as though it were dictated from the celestial blueprint, with no effort from him. There was the overture written the night before the premiere, the three last symphonies written in a few weeks one summer. Music flowed out of his mind like water from a spring, clear, transparent, and of exquisite taste. The show-piece cadenzas of the many piano concerti, improvised for his own performances as a traveling soloist, had the structural integrity of calculated symphonic architecture. The development sections of his sonatas and chamber music have an abandonment and verve, improvisatory in essence. His operas are looked upon as consummate musical theater, having the right balance of dramatic recitative with contemplative arias and vital culminating ensemble scenes. If Bach was the musical giant of the Baroque, Mozart was the spontaneous genius of the Age of Enlightenment. In spite of his early death at the age of thirty-five, his prodigious output was over six hundred works. But quantity is only one aspect to elicit our amazement. A high order of quality marked virtually the entire output of his incandescently creative mind.

Ludwig van Beethoven was the great deaf romantic who stormed the heavens with defiance of his fate, who dialogued with God in the Missa Solemnis and the A-minor string quartet, singing the brotherhood of all humanity in the chorale finale of the Ninth Symphony. If Mozart was able to conceive a whole flawless symphony in a matter of a few days, Beethoven spent twelve years polishing and perfecting one theme. His voluminous sketchbooks vividly depict his wrestling with the evolution and convolution of his themes and their development. He was forever seeking the right note, the right chord, the right rhythm, frequently not being satisfied with the first version, the fifth version, or the fourteenth. The search was relentless. He gave himself little rest until he was assured that he had the best possible solution to a musical problem of a given work, movement, or passage. His quest for perfection in each composition can be likened to the sculptor who envisions a beautiful bust in the heart of a block of granite. He chips away at the stone until the image emerges, first in rough textured form, then continuing until the smooth, balanced lines become the reality of his mental creation. Beethoven knew that somewhere in the series of notes, rhythms, and chords was the perfected image of that particular movement, and he would continue to chip away until his critical judgment confirmed that it was right.

Each of these three musical masters is different, yet they had one important facet in common. The musical vision that each possessed was so clear, so positive, so beautiful, so excellent, that to change one note is not so much musical heresy as it is, in fact, ludicrous. Their music needs no addition, no subtraction, no padding, no explanation. Their music has something in common with the creations of God in that it presents to us a paradox. It is at once immediately accessible and ultimately unfathomable. It thrills our souls, but we cannot say why. We cannot probe the essence of music that causes spiritual ecstasy. But what we can come away with is the feeling that we have come face to face with a beautiful and valuable human experience that is also related to the divine.

Excellence of musical substance and in the manipulation of musical elements by the composers is indeed the common denominator of the masterworks of Bach, Mozart, and Beethoven. While their musical styles and rhetoric are varied, communicative power and excellence permeate virtually every bar of the music of all three.

As I observe the standard of excellence in the works of Deity and in the works of human genius, I find myself desiring its stamp on my own lesser activity, for the purpose of enjoying the satisfaction that accompanies it. Excellence puts its hallmark on any activity we engage in if we demand of ourselves those pains and that time and imposition of talent and intelligence in adequate measure to insure quality.

May I present two illustrations on the thrust toward excellence that are part of my own musical experience. The first comes from my work as a composer of the *Symphony No. 2, Music for the Hill Cumorah Pageant,* for chorus and orchestra. I have recounted elsewhere how I became involved in preparing the musical score to this epic dramatic vehicle, which is given annually on the slopes of the Hill Cumorah, twenty-two miles from Rochester, New York. Here I wish to refer to the problem of achieving excellence in this musical endeavor. The Hill Cumorah Pageant proclaims a second witness for Jesus Christ. The accompanying music called for profundity, an ingredient that one cannot manufacture, cannot fake, cannot use a substitute for. Its presence in art is unmistakable; its absence, when needed, is virtually inexcusable, at least from the artistic point of view.

I labored with the Christ theme, which is central to the Hill Cumorah music, for several years, even to the point of making up an orchestral score and set of parts for the BYU symphony and a cappella choir to record a trial run. If I recall correctly, I wrote fifteen or more versions of the Christ theme prior to that recording. But when it was done and I listened to it, I knew it was not good enough. The next version was then approached, with additional fasting and prayer, with trips to the temple, and with a special blessing from Harold B. Lee, then a member of the Twelve, who was significantly associated with the pageant. I had no delusions about my stature as a composer. I was not among the masters, or even close. But I was the one whom the Lord had called to fulfill this function, and he expected me to fulfill it with excellence. I was determined to do just that.

The spiritual experience associated with composing the Christ theme was personal enough to omit here. But I refer to it in order to suggest that, in addition to our own diligent intensity of effort, the striving for excellence often requires amplification from the Lord. The deadline for recording the music drew near, and I had not yet completed composing the hour-long score. There was no possibility of changing the date, for the Salt Lake Tabernacle, the Utah Symphony, and the BYU choirs had all been booked long in advance in order to be available for those chosen few days in 1957. There was the problem of maintaining excellence in the music under tremendous pressure, as well as in the mechanics of preparing the music for use by the orchestra members and singers. The latter involved a complex pattern of technical steps that began with my initial rough sketch of musical ideas and continued to the completed orchestral-choral score. At this point the copyists began copying the orchestral parts and proofreading for each other, and finally the full score and the extracted instrumental and vocal parts were printed. There was a constant possibility of error or omission. We worked out elaborate procedures to avoid or at least minimize errors that would damage and delay the precious and limited rehearsal and recording time.

With the assistance of a hard-working and devoted

team of copyists, a fairly high degree of technical excellence was achieved in the mechanical preparation of the score and parts. A similar story could be told concerning the recording technicians and the musicians, whose cooperative efforts combined to achieve a technically excellent recording.

Striving for excellence was the hallmark of this project. I am too close to the Cumorah music to assess accurately the degree of musical excellence present, but what I do wish to communicate is my commitment to the concept of the pursuit of excellence.

Looking back to my student years, I recall another experience that has set a standard of excellence in my conducting activities. I had the privilege of studying orchestral conducting under Maurice Faulkner, a singularly charismatic teacher who steps out of my memory in brilliant colors. His class had the reputation for being the hardest in the music curriculum. In addition to studying texts and engaging in the usual classroom drills, we had firing-line experience in conducting the second-level bands, orchestras, and choral groups for laboratory work and as apprentices. The course included instruction in how to learn an orchestral score so it could be conducted from memory. Normally this requirement is found only on the graduate level among students who anticipate careers in conducting, but Professor Faulkner expected it of his undergraduate music students.

The final examination under Professor Faulkner is still, decades later, most vivid in my mind. He had assigned each of us to prepare a movement of the Beethoven Symphony no. 4, a chorus from the *Messiah,* and the Tschaikovsky "Romeo and Juliet Fantasy Overture." One of these was selected for each student as he was invited to the podium before an imaginary orchestra to conduct that piece while Faulkner played the recorded music. I recall the cold, clammy feeling I got as I stepped onto the podium in the empty room. Professor Faulkner sat with arms folded as though to say, "Show me if you can do anything with this assignment." He dropped the needle on a recording of the Tschaikovsky *Romeo and Juliet.* The piece begins with a quartet of two bassoons and two clarinets. Before the passage had hardly progressed, he picked up the needle and asked me, "Where are we?" I told him the measure number calculated by the phrase size and shape from the beginning. "What is playing?" I described the quartet. "What key are we in?" "F-sharp minor." "What is the second bassoon playing on the next downbeat? What dynamics? What is the name of the sonority?" etc., etc. Down came the needle, and for twenty seconds or so I conducted my imaginary orchestra, following the recording until the needle came off again. The questions continued on a large number of technical details. I answered some, while some I could not answer. I kept thinking "What an impossible examination! How can anyone ever know an orchestral score so thoroughly as to be able to answer all those questions from memory? One would have to have a photographic mind to be able to recall that kind of minutia."

I don't know how long I was on the podium or how many needle drops there were, but I do know I was completely wrung out when it was over. What has remained with me to this day is the standard of excellence in conducting study and preparation that Maurice Faulkner set for me. Each of the thousands of times I have mounted the podium since that early lonely day, I have recalled the ideal I learned from that one exam—to have learned the score so well that I no longer need it for reference. Its notation, its architectonics, its style, its traditional performance practices, its printing errors, and a host of other details are known to me. If I can invest the time for this kind of mastery, then my appearance in front of a symphony or choir or in an opera performance can be executed with eye-to-eye contact with my colleagues without that barrier of the music stand and score. I can address, in advance, the sections and soloists, thus providing them assurance of the precise location and musical character of their entrances. These things can be done and are done by conductors of much greater stature than I with the use of the score, so I do not wish to enter into a shadow-boxing exercise with anyone over the relative merits of using a score or not. But for me, it is a huge advantage to have this substantial knowledge safely stored in my memory so my full energy, attention, and concentration can be devoted to the unfettered communication with my musical colleagues.

At this writing it has been my blessing to have achieved this type of recall for over three hundred orchestral, operatic, orchestral-choral, and ballet works, including a substantial body of the major repertory for orchestra. All this goes back to Maurice Faulkner's conducting class. He taught me excellence in preparation, excellence in score study and analysis, excellence in mental, aural, and visual recall, and excellence in communication as a conductor projecting my own vision of the musical message of the composer at hand. The standard still seems impossibly high and extremely hard, but the effort to reach for it has given me deep satisfaction. There have been many moments when the communication has been locked in between the players and myself and we have come close to the ideal. The visual image of the pages has flown by in my mind, accompanied by the sound registering bar by bar, beat by beat, just ahead of the actual sound being produced by the musicians. The postured standard has fulfilled its purpose. It has caused me to reach high for the ultimate achievement of calling forth all of my intellectual, emotional, and spiritual resources, and I have found that striving for that standard is an exercise of exceedingly great worth. When the players and I are one, and the audience senses the unity and responds to the message being presented in such magical moments, I say to myself, "This is one reason why I am alive—to help create such moments of human communication and joy!"

The pursuit of excellence does bring rich rewards. It reminds us of our God-like aspirations. It reminds us that we are engaged in a process that great geniuses of many disciplines have invoked in their own work, to the blessing of us all. It promises us deep and abiding satisfaction in our work if we invite its yoke upon ourselves as we dream, plan, work, create, and communicate.

Crawford Gates, an award-winning composer, is artist in residence and professor of music at Beloit College in Wisconsin. He is also music director of the Be-

loit Janesville Symphony Orchestra and the Rockford Symphony Orchestra. Previously he was chairman of the department of music at Brigham Young University. He has some 650 arrangements or compositions to his credit, as well as over one hundred music publications. He received a B.A. from California State University at San Jose, an M.A. from BYU, and a Ph.D. from the Eastman School of Music at the University of Rochester. In the Church he has served as a bishop, high councilor, member of the general music committee, and member of the Young Men's Mutual Improvement Association general board. He and his wife, the former Georgia Lauper, have four children.

THE TIES THAT BIND:
A FOUNDATION OF EXCELLENCE

Reba L. Keele

Some years ago I was participating with several colleagues in a selection interview for a prestigious scholarship. Before us was a young man with a most impressive vita—pages and pages of extracurricular activites and publications to go along with his high grade-point average. One of the faculty asked him, "What did you give up to build this impressive vita?" The answer was a powerful lesson for us. The young man began to sob and finally replied, "My friends, my family, and my health."

By all the measures any of us in the room were used to using as standards, this young man was an exemplar of excellence. He brought goal setting and achievement to a high form of planning. He had started to work on winning those awards six years earlier, and had directed everything toward becoming excellent academically and in service activities. But when asked, he knew immediately that the cost was too high, that somehow he had missed the mark, that excellence had other dimensions that also needed a focus or it could not be achieved.

We often take for granted the existence of relationships in our lives, assuming that they can flourish and grow (or at least remain stable) without time and effort being devoted to them. I believe that no search for excellence will ultimately succeed unless it includes a commitment to and devotion of time to building a strong support system.

What is a support system? It is a network composed of all those people who offer to any individual what is called in the sociological literature "social support." One writer has said, "Social support is an expression of the ongoing interdependence between people; mutuality is its cornerstone. . . . Social support consists of verbal and/or nonverbal information or advice, tangible aid, or action that is proffered by social intimates . . . and has beneficial emotional or behavioral effects on the recipient."[1] The person who has family, friends, business associates, or neighbors will not automatically have a good support system. Each relationship has the power to be stressful as well as supportive, and the mere existence of persons who fit certain categories does not mean that they are more supportive than stressful, or that we have been successful in building a support system. A support system exists only when enough time and effort have been invested that the relationships are more supportive than stressful. The importance of an adequate support system cannot be exaggerated. A growing body of research indicates that it was not accidental that our devastated student linked the loss of friends and family to his loss of health. There are real and serious consequences of isolation, which has been demonstrated by both animal and human studies.

James House summarizes much of the animal research in his book *Work Stress and Social Support.*[2] Animals as diverse as goats, rats, mice, and rabbits have all been found to experience health effects from aversive stimuli administered to them alone that are different from the effects in conflict situations administered in the presence of littermates, parents, or caring humans. Lynch's summary of the research on dogs and horses shows the immense effect of human presence and touch on the physiological responses of the animals.[3] While it is possible with animals to directly measure the effects of various treatments, it is much more difficult to do so with humans. However, some studies have been instructive, if not conclusive, about the mechanisms that protect humans from the negative effects of stress when they are in the presence of someone from their support system.

When a catheter was placed in blood vessels of students and they were then subjected to a stress experiment where their judgment was questioned, the amount of free fatty acid in their blood increased—unless they were participating with friends. The effect was lessened even if the people they were with were only those with whom they had taken a test the day before.[4]

Surgical patients given supportive care by the anesthetist went home an average of 2.7 days earlier and received substantially less pain medication than the control group.[5] Pregnant women experiencing high stress with low social support experienced birth complications in 91 percent of the cases, while women with equally high stress but with high support experienced them in only 33 percent of the cases, lower even than the 39 percent experienced by women with low stress.[6]

The sudden loss of a partner, especially if one does not have another confidant, may result in the death of the surviving spouse soon after the separation.[7] The presence or absence of four kinds of social ties—marriage, friends, church membership, and informal or formal group memberships—explained the death rates of those in Alameda County, California. People low or lacking in each type of social tie were from 30 percent to 300 percent more likely to die than those who had each type of relationship.[8]

I could continue to pile up the evidence, ranging from the effects of unemployment to drinking. There seems to be little need. The evidence is clear that it is healthier to be involved with people than not to be; that it is not just "nice" to have friends, but perhaps essential for our physical and psychological well-being. Any plan of excellence that ignores relationships is ignoring the human condition. Even the uniquely human attribute of language, with all its ambiguity and ability to communicate many layers of meaning, has as its outcome the relatedness of human beings.[9] I infer from the body of evidence that it makes a real difference in our lives when we have enmeshed ourselves in a network of support. I have come to understand better the complex relationships that were being expressed by the young man who gave up friends, family, and health—the former may indeed have caused the latter.

Claude Fischer has noted that "individuals are linked to their society primarily through relations with other individuals: with kin, friends, co-workers, fellow club members, and so on. We are each the center of a web of social bonds that radiates outward to the people whom we know intimately, those whom we know well, those whom we know casually, and to the wider society beyond. These are our personal social networks. Society affects us largely through tugs on the strands of our networks—shaping our attitudes, providing opportunities, making demands on us and so forth. And it is by tugging at those same strands that we make our individual impacts on society—influencing other people's opinions, obtaining favors from insiders, forming action groups."[10]

The role of relationships in excellence is central. It is through relationships that we develop, demonstrate, and evaluate excellence in ourselves and others. As Fischer makes clear, we accomplish most of what we accomplish through influencing others. The ability to influence others depends not only upon expertise and competence in a chosen speciality, but also upon our ability to exercise those skills for the benefit of others. I am not talking about a calculated establishing of relationship because it meets our needs, but rather a loving attention to those with whom we interact—a compassionate, nonjudgmental recognition of all that they can teach us. What are some of the particular ways that relationships help us toward excellence in our lives?

One of the first and most important aids to excellence is the learning that comes from interaction with others, whether teachers or peers. The importance and role of teachers is self-evident. Less obvious is the value of peer relationships at every stage of learning. Lewis Thomas describes his experience in medical school: "When I am asked . . . which member of the Harvard faculty had the greatest influence on my education in medicine, I no longer grope for a name on that distinguished roster. What I remember now, from this distance, is the influence of my classmates. We taught each other; we may even have set careers for each other without realizing at the time that so fundamental an educational process was even going on. I am not so troubled as I used to be by the need to reform the medical school curriculum. What worries me these days is that the curriculum, whatever its sequential arrangement, has become so crowded with lectures and seminars, with such masses of data to be learned, that the students may not be having enough time to instruct each other in what may lie ahead."[11]

The work of learning requires others to balance the solitary work that is always part of the foundation of excellence. We learn by bouncing ideas off each other, by trying to defend new ideas, by being led to see weaknesses in our arguments or understanding, by considering the ethics of trying to convince others to believe or perceive as we do. Learning requires both the commitment to spending time alone mastering something and the sharing of that which we have mastered with others who are part of our social network—tugging on the strands of our network, in Fischer's terms.

How quickly and easily we forget that we share more with others than we differ from them. A focus on excellence that does not also focus on relationships becomes a focus on differences and allows for the real possibility of elitism and a sense of being better than others. We share not just a biological commonality, but also an experiential one, no matter how different our life may be from that of those around us. It is that process of discovering commonalities that explains why the parents of teenagers have learned so much by the time the teenager turns twenty-one! One example expressed in early Utah by Lucy Hannah White Flake shows the effects of understanding shared experience. Sister Flake is discussing being required to move from Lehi to Cedar City: "Until now these moves had been more in the nature of an adventure to me, something new and exciting. Now I began to sense my mother's feelings, her sorrow in leaving home and loved ones. I had some schoolmates whom I loved very much. I couldn't see why we should have to go into the wilderness once more and begin all over again. Many a night I cried myself to sleep, from sheer homesickness, and it drew me closer to mother."[12]

Only as we learn to understand the feelings of others do

we learn how to apply the excellence we have obtained to the service of others. The danger is that we become like the people Neal A. Maxwell described at a Brigham Young University convocation on May 29, 1970: "As we know each other less well, it is more and more difficult for us to trust each other; it is also easier for us to stereotype others, and it is easier for us to polarize our viewpoints. Somehow, in ways we do not fully understand, while density and complexity crowd us together they also tend to separate us. When we are spiritually and experientially separated it is paradoxically easier to believe the worst about others rather than the best about them. In the Moffatt version of First Corinthians, chapter 13, Paul says: 'Love is never glad when others go wrong.' This kind of perverted gladness occurs more frequently when we do not really know each other, when we have labeled and categorized others, when we merely brush against others instead of coming to understand them, and when we know each other as functions rather than people."

Remembering that no excellence can be claimed unless it also contributes to the lives of others in some way will help us to avoid labeling, categorizing, and oversimplifying those with whom we associate.

No matter the level of excellence each of us achieves, we do so by compensating for and gradually overcoming weaknesses. The importance of being able to lean upon others who have strengths that match our weaknesses ought to be self-evident, but unfortunately it is not. How many times do we become discouraged in our search for individual excellence because we don't know how to turn to others to balance our lopsided efforts? Are we are defeated by weaknesses that need not have proved fatal? We are neither self-sufficient nor able to be so. Throughout literature we find many descriptions of friendships that allowed both parties to become more than they might have been without each other. One such relationship is described in Willa Cather's *Death Comes for the Archbishop,* [13] in which we see the cool, critical, hard-to-please, gray-in-mood LaTour balanced by the intense, rash, fervently faithful, and totally dedicated Vaillant. Together they are able to accomplish much in the early history of New Mexico that would not have been accomplished by either one alone. Each of us can think of friendships at some point in our lives that helped us to be more than we are or could be alone.

Those who balance us do not even have to be close friends. Many people we barely know are able to serve as role models or to give needed information. We need only look for those who offer balance. The best boss is one who has the confidence and skill to hire those who do well the things the boss does less well. The least successful is one who can hire only those who are less capable so that they are not threatening.

Our networks provide many kinds of support for us. James House has classified them most usefully, in my opinion.[14] He says that we give and receive four kinds of support. These are:

1. *Emotional.* This is a sense that we are important and that others are concerned about us. This may be the most important kind of support, and the type that has the most health effects. Many of us are quite good at giving emotional support, not very good at receiving it, and terrible at asking for support. Emotional support requires some continuing presence or sense of togetherness, whether personally, by telephone, or by letter. Some years ago I did a Special Interest workshop in California, and asked the women in the group what their greatest fear was. One said (and others nodded all around the room), "I'm afraid I'll die and no one will know for two weeks." Those sisters lacked emotional support, and clearly the structures of the Church designed to provide that support were not working for them. All of us need a sense that our passing would make a difference to someone, that someone is concerned.

2. *Appraisal.* This is feedback, social comparisons, and reality checking. Appraisal information helps us decide how we are doing compared to others or to a standard. Many of us find it difficult to ask others for appraisal information unless they are very close friends. That is typically a mistake. We sometimes make the error of believing that the most important standards we are compared against are those in our pro-

fession or speciality. Continually being able to see how far we have come as well as how far we have still to go will help us keep perspective about the appropriateness of the standards against which we are judging ourselves. I have always found it compelling that the Lord describes those in the celestial kingdom as those who "see as they are seen, and know as they are known" (D&C 76:94), which must indeed be the ultimate in appraisal support. What better description is there of excellence than to know how we are seen and known and to see and know ourselves in the same way that others do?

3. *Informational.* We need other kinds of information than appraisal information to be excellent. To know where resources can be found, who can help, what is the best approach to take, how to approach someone to ask for help— all of these and more are essential for achieving excellence or achieving support. People are our best sources of information about most things, and the more people we know, the more sources of information we have.

4. *Instrumental.* This is the kind of support that comes from another person's being able to modify our environment in some way, such as in provision of time, money, aid, or intervention in the environment in some way. For all of us, having others on whom we can call for this kind of support is essential—it is a part of the learning together I talked about earlier, a part of the service that wasn't being done for those Special Interest members in California. It is the crux of service to others, and without excellence in this area we cannot wholly claim excellence anywhere else in our network.

These four kinds of support are the foundations of our relationships with others. It is highly unlikely that any one person, even a spouse, can always provide all four kinds of support for another person; typically we need to have a broad base of relationships to have all of those needs met all of the time. How do we go about building the relationships that provide support and allow us to be excellent in service as well as in accomplishments?

George Kneller has written: "Every person needs to participate in the life of others. If he retires into himself, he frustrates his own development, forcing his energies back on themselves, so that they rend him in tensions and neuroses. If, on the other hand, he empties and disperses himself in others, conforming to their expectations, he betrays his uniqueness and fails to realize his potentialities. Consciously or not, he loses the will and courage to be himself. Flight in the self, flight out of it—both are equally sterile."[15]

Knowing that one must participate in the life of others and knowing how to do so effectively are not the same thing. To walk that line between doing what others wish and turning into oneself requires conscious attention, an investment of time, and a commitment to relationships. How might we begin the process of building a network? Here are five keys:

1. *Evaluate our areas of weakness.* The first step is to look at the kinds of support each of us needs and then to list those people who provide each kind of support. Do we feel as if the amount of support we receive in each area is adequate? If not, is it because too few people provide that particular type of support, or because we have placed unrealistic expectations on the people who are there, and they have failed to meet them? It is also instructive to list the people to whom we *give* each type of support.

2. *Determine possible additions.* Second, we can each make a list of the people who might be additions to our network. These might be people who have made overtures previously, people we know who know information we need, organizations involved in doing work we are interested in, or people we have wanted to contact for whatever reason.

3. *Determine what we have to offer.* All human relationships are based on the principle of reciprocity—that is, we do not persist in a relationship from which we do not gain as well as give. One of the biggest barriers to reaching out to others is the perception that we have nothing to offer to them, and thus would only be receiving. It is a useful exercise to write down personal strengths, including those growing out of accomplishments and those growing out of character traits. Without a sense of having something to offer others, it is unlikely that anyone can do other than turn inward.

4. *Commit time and energy to relationships.* No relationships can be initiated, let alone nurtured, without a willingness to consider time spent on relationships as valuable and worthwhile time. Quality of time is more important than quantity, but some minimum amount of time must be spent for two people to build the amount of trust essential for reciprocity to develop. Not everyone who provides support needs to be a close, personal friend—information can come from the friend of a friend of a cousin—but most people aren't willing to invest unless they feel some equal amount of investment coming back.

5. *Be willing to share ourselves.* A willingness to allow others to know what we need, what we have to offer, and what we want is an essential step in building a network. Sidney J. Jourard writes: "I suspect that a man's life begins to lose in meaning most rapidly when he becomes estranged from his fellows, when they become strangers to him and when he lets himself become a stranger to them; when he distrusts others so much he misleads them into thinking they know him when, in fact, he knows that they do not and cannot." He explains: "You cannot love another person, that is, behave toward him so as to foster his happiness and growth, unless you know what he needs. And you cannot know what he needs unless he tells you. How can you know him, and he you, unless you have engaged in enough mutual disclosure of self to be able to anticipate how he will react and what part he will play?"[16]

The more diversity there is in our networks, the more likely that our support needs and our need to give support will be met. Humans are very diverse—our biology guarantees that—and this testifies to the value our Creator must feel for differences. Often we try to annihilate differences rather than integrate them, and feel uncomfortable in the presence of those who differ from ourselves, whatever those differences are. The only sin some people can never forgive in others is a difference of opinion!

The need to act now rather than later and the barriers to action are identified by George Kneller: "Each of us is a

unique pattern of potentialities; each of us gives to and re-
ceives from life something that will never be repeated.
Moreover, each of us must either mold himself or allow external circumstances to mold him. The choice must be made
again and again throughout our lives. Hence, time is the spur
to achievement. The days slip by irretrievably; we must act.
The three great enemies of action are ignorance, fear, and
lack of confidence."[17]

Excellence depends upon overcoming ignorance, fear,
and lack of confidence. Ignorance cannot be our excuse, fear
is overcome by the teachings of Christ, and confidence is
built by trying in small steps and tasting success. A social
network is essential to growth and excellence. Discipline
and hard work that are applied only to accomplishments and
not to relationships result in empty victories and resounding
defeats. The prices are too high when we sacrifice the ties
that bind for success in anything else.

[1]Benjamin Gottlieb, *Social Support Strategies: Guidelines for Mental Health Practice,* vol. 7, Sage Studies in Community Mental Health (Beverly Hills: Sage Publications, 1983), pp. 28-29.

[2]James S. House, *Work, Stress, and Social Support* (Menlo Park, Calif.: Addison-Wesley Publishing Co., 1981), pp. 44-46.

[3]James J. Lynch, *The Broken Heart: The Medical Consequences of Loneliness* (New york: Basic Books, Inc., 1979), pp. 167-80.

[4]K. W. Back and M. D. Bogdonoff, "Buffer Conditions in Experimental Stress," *Behavioral Science* 12 (1967): 384-90. Cited in House, *op. cit.,* p. 46.

[5]L. D. Egbert et al., "Reduction of Post-Operative Pain by Encouragement and Instruction of Patients," *New England Journal of Medicine* 270 (1964): 825-27.

[6]K. B. Nuckolls et al., "Psychosocial Assets, Life, Crisis, and the Prognosis of Pregnancy," *American Journal of Epidemiology* 95 (1972): 431-41.

[7]Lynch, *op. cit,* pp. 55-121.

[8]L. F. Berkman and S. L. Syme, "Social Networks, Host Resistance, and Mortality: A Nine-Year Follow-up of Alameda County Residents," *American Journal of Epidemiology* 109: 186-204. Cited in House, *op. cit.,* p. 52.

[9]Lewis Thomas, *The Lives of a Cell: Notes of a Biology Watcher* (New York: Bantam Books, Inc., 1974), pp. 104-12.

[10]Claude Fischer, quoted in Laura Lein, "The Ties That Bind: An Introduction," *Marriage and Family Review* 5 (1982): 3-7.

[11]Lewis Thomas, *The Youngest Science: Notes of a Medicine Watcher* (New York: Bantam Books, 1983), pp. 29-30.

¹²Lucy Hannah White Flake Journal, typescript, Brigham Young University, p. 9.

¹³Willa Cather, *Death Comes for the Archbishop* (New York: Vintage Books, 1971).

¹⁴House, *op. cit.*

¹⁵George F. Kneller, *The Art and Science of Creativity* (New York: Holt, Rinehart and Winston, 1965), p. 94.

¹⁶Sidney J. Jourard, *The Transparent Self* (New York: D. Van Nostrand Co., Inc., 1964), pp. iv, iii.

¹⁷Kneller, *op. cit.*, p. 89.

Reba L. Keele is director of the Center for Women's Health at the Cottonwood Hospital Medical Center in Murray, Utah, and a member of the Utah System of Higher Education Board of Regents. Previously she was associate professor of organizational behavior in the Graduate School of Management and director of the honors program at Brigham Young University. She was named Honors Professsor of the Year in 1982-83 and received the Karl G. Maeser Distinguished Teaching Award in 1983. In 1975 Dr. Keele was named Outstanding Young Woman in Utah. She received an associate degree from the College of Eastern Utah, her bachelor's and master's degrees from Brigham Young University, and a Ph.D. in speech communications from Purdue University.

INDEX